BATTLE CRY

BATTLE CRY

Waging the spiritual battle for your prodigal

LOVE GOES TO WAR

CR

ST JOSEPH, MISSOURI USA

BATTLE CRY: Waging the spiritual battle for your prodigal
Copyright © 2024 Debra McNinch
ISBN: 978-1-936501-93-9

Unless otherwise indicated, all Scriptures from the Holy Bible, English Standard Version, copyright © 2001, 2007, 2011, 2016 by Crossway Bibles, a division of Good News Publishers. Used by permission. All rights reserved.

Scripture quotations marked MSG are taken from THE MESSAGE, copyright © 1993, 2002, 2018 by Eugene H. Peterson. Used by permission of NavPress, represented by Tyndale House Publishers. All rights reserved.

Scripture taken from the New King James Version®. Copyright © 1982 by Thomas Nelson. Used by permission. All rights reserved.

DISCLAIMER: This book is not intended as a substitute for the professional advice of counselors or therapists. The reader should consult a professional in matters relating to his/her mental health and particularly with respect to any symptoms that may require diagnosis or medical attention.

For more information on Debra McNinch, visit DebraMcNinch.com

Editor: Debra L. Butterfield
Cover Design: Tamara Clymer
Cover art: Photo 73882663 | Rainbow © Cammeraydave | Dreamstime.com
Printed in the United States of America

To all the parents in a 1 Samuel 1:10 season.

CONTENTS

ACKNOWLEDGEMENTS

Thank you to all who made my writing dream come true.

My adventure partner of more than 30 years, Steve. I love my fairytale.

My children. My entire world. There are not enough words to say how much I love you. I look forward to eating with you at the Marriage Supper of the Lamb.

My mama. Thank you for teaching me to fight for what I believe in. I miss you.

My Exodus 17:12–13 friends who have walked with me on this journey.

Becky and Tami, I could not do life without you both.

Lea and Shawn, thank you for loving us.

Heather, Steph, Tricia, Heather, Jolynne, and Lara. My tribe. I love you.

Kelly, my Northern bestie. Thank you for your never-ending support.

Telisa, Amy, Sarah, Suzy, Becca, Fran, Nicole, Audrey, and my Bible Party Girls! Thank you for the texts of support, prayers as I would write, and your love.

My BATTLECRY family...NO ONE FIGHTS ALONE

I would also like to thank those who built my strong faith in Christ. I would not be who I am without those who poured into me! It is because of you my foundation is strong.

Central Baptist Church.

Central Baptist Youth group.

Randy, Sharon, RD…You will never know, this side of heaven, the impact you have had on my life.

Mr. B…Thank you for being the best teacher ever and teaching me to love writing.

Mostly, I would like to give praise to Jesus. You are worthy of all my praise.

"Behold, I am coming soon." - Jesus

INTRODUCTION

"HOW TO BE THE BEST CHRISTIAN MOM" …that's the
the book I thought I would write. So you might say the title
was a shock. In fact, this book could have been called, "Motherhood, it isn't for the weak: How to miscalculate everything,
become jealous of all your friends, and never forgive yourself."

Years ago, a friend prophesied a Rachel anointing over my
life. I had no idea what that meant. Like any prophetic word,
I filed it away and carried it in my heart, wondering when it
would make sense. More than a decade went by before the
meaning became clear.

Last year, I spent my warm summer days reading and re-
reading the Gospels—focusing on Jesus and His life. Every day I
poured through the accounts of my favorite chapters in the Bible.

My third time through Matthew, a verse flew off the page.

"A voice was heard in Ramah, weeping and loud lamentation, Rachel weeping for her children; she refused to be comforted, because they are no more" (Matthew 2:18).

Confession time…I've read that verse a million times and
never really paid attention. I wanted to get on to the good
stuff…angels, shepherds, wisemen…all the exciting parts of
the story. Sure, I knew Herod ordered all the babies under two

years old to be killed, and there was great sadness, but I never understood who Rachel was or cared enough to look for more.

But on this day, I decided to dig a little deeper, and I discovered the verse fulfilled a prophecy from Jeremiah.

"Thus says the LORD: 'A voice heard in Ramah, lamentation and bitter weeping. Rachel is weeping for her children; she refuses to be comforted for her children, because they are no more" (Jeremiah 31:15).

I knew Rachel was the mother of Joseph and Benjamin, two of the twelve tribes of Israel. But why couldn't she be comforted?

Because the prophet saw the people of Israel being dragged into captivity, and Rachel wept the loss of promises and broken dreams. As the tribes walked into exile, they passed by her grave. Rachel's weeping was a picture of extreme grief over the loss of a nation. Just as the verse in Matthew expresses grief over the slaughter of innocent babies, we see here the loss of what her family and nation would look like. Rachel's children...her dreams, her future, her hopes...all gone.

I can understand that. I had dreams, hopes and plans. Yet, just like Rachel, things changed drastically.

REFUSING

Like the nation in Jeremiah's day, our children are being held captive by the lies of Satan himself. Kids wander farther away from biblical values every day, and it feels like there is nothing we can do.

As I read, studied, and meditated on that verse...and then prayed about it, I finally realized what the Rachel anointing means.

I needed to *refuse* to be comforted.

I didn't have to fall in line and accept the world's lies. I did not have to believe the myths the church was telling me. I had a choice. I could *refuse* to be comforted. Refuse to believe our kids' futures are out of God's control. My heavenly Father invited me to trust Him and not settle for anything less than seeing my kids come home.

I had a choice to make…would I accept that a generation is falling away and write it off as kids being kids, or would I step into what God was calling me to do—refuse to be comforted and believe that my kids will come home?

I found the answer to that question right there in Jeremiah…"Thus says the LORD: 'Keep your voice from weeping, and your eyes from tears, for there is a reward for your work, declares the LORD, and they shall come back from the land of the enemy. There is hope for your future, declares the LORD, and your children shall come back to their own country'" (Jer. 31:16–17).

The decision was mine. I needed to lay aside every dream, every hope, every plan I had as a parent and completely surrender to the Lord to move forward. The Lord was telling me…

Forget your plans and trust in Mine. This road will be hard. You will have people talk about you. You will be unfriended. You will be labeled unfairly and misunderstood. You will want to quit and believe what the world says, because it will be the easier path.

Do not quit.

Keep your eyes on Me. You will feel the struggle between worldliness and godliness like never before. I am raising you up as a connector and cheerleader. Use the pain from your circumstances to unite others going through their own great loss and encourage them to keep going.

The words in this book were hard to put on paper. I hate that I had to write them. I hate even more that you are reading them. I hate that Satan comes to steal, kill, and destroy, and that somehow, he's managed to ambush our families.

Yet…

This is a word I love. Even though all these things have invaded our family over the last few years, *yet*…I am reminded daily that we serve a God who is calm in the chaos and makes beauty from ashes. He knows the end from the beginning and nothing is a surprise. *Yet*…the story is not over. *Yet*…God's promises are true, and He will fulfill every one of them in His time. *Yet*…there is hope.

My prayer is that as you read this book, you will realize you are not alone. And if you have children who are walking with the Lord, please join us in praying for our prodigals.

Mostly, I hope you will see this not as a story of despair but one of hope!

I decided early in my journey that Satan might steal things from me but joy would not be one of them. When he came after my family, he miscalculated the mama bear he picked on.

I hope this story will make you laugh, cry a little, but mostly lead you to pray harder and with more passion than you ever have before.

The countdown to the return of Christ is on. We don't have the luxury of time. We need to believe and pray for our kids to come home to Jesus, today! Please join me in standing on the porch, watching the horizon, waiting to see them return.

The war is on and we will not lose. Satan will not get our kids.

1. THE FAIRYTALE

ONCE UPON A TIME...

Aww...I love how all great fairy tales start.

As a little girl, I read the story of Cinderella every day. I still have the original book from my childhood on display in my home. I remember studying the colorful pages, letting my imagination tell the story long before I could read the words. Each way I imagined it, the story ended the same:

And they lived happily ever after.

I still love fairytales. They make me happy. I can hardly read any other type of book. That's probably why I read books the way I do.

I read the first chapter, then flip to the end. I skim the words, looking for the main characters' names. I have to know how their story ends. I need to make sure everyone pulls through. That nobody dies. That love happens. That the family is still together. I have to be certain my heart won't get broken into a thousand pieces.

I fast-forward through all the suspense so I can learn the outcome. Knowing it will end well, reassures me during the middle—the place of questions, pain, uncertainty, doubt, confusion, and loneliness. I can manage the middle when I know the story ends with a happily ever after.

The same is true for Bible stories I've read a hundred times. I do a quick memory check of all the story details to double-check the ending before I even start. I have to remind my heart that God always has a plan, and when the enemy comes against His people, God already has the victory.

This might sound crazy to those of you who don't have control issues, but somehow, I think I can manipulate what happens along the way if I know the outcome. Although it may speak less about my control issues and more about my heart issues.

The story of David and Goliath is one of my favorites. A small shepherd boy, a mighty giant, a slingshot…all enough to make my heart skip a beat in suspense. Even though I know the outcome because I have the complete story, I remind myself that on that day, David didn't know.

He did not know when he left to deliver food to his brothers that he would face a mighty enemy of Israel. He was not prepared in all the ways the world would expect, but in his heart, he was ready. He didn't need to know how big the giant was because he knew how big his God was. He didn't need to know the end of the story because leaving the outcome to the One who authors our stories was enough for him.

Oh, how I long to have that kind of faith. Faith big enough to believe that any Goliath that comes my way is no match for the God I serve…the same God that rescued David.

If only life could be like that. If only we could get just a glimpse of what the end of our stories are like, so when the tough times come, we can know for certain it will all work out.

PASSPORT STAMPS

Imagine if, when you became a parent, they handed you a magical passport. It would be something you could flip through to see all the places your parenting journey would take you. There would be stamps for stops for soccer games, family vacations, birthday parties, proms, and graduations. It would be a glimpse of all the fun ahead of you, and all the amazing places parenting travels lead.

Of course, you would get all the perfect stamps that show the perfect life and you wouldn't have to worry about whether it would all work out because it would be right there in your book. You could flip to the end anytime you wanted to reassure yourself that the perfect ending to your perfect life was waiting.

Unfortunately, real life doesn't work like that magic passport. You don't get to know the whole story in advance. Real life gives you one day at a time and requires real time faith. Parenting struggles come every day, and you learn how to trust God through them each step of the way.

In living my parenting book, I was on chapter twenty-three before my faith was truly tested. Each chapter up until that point was beautiful. We filled each page with happiness, joy, and anticipation of the future. When we finally escaped the kids' teenage years, I set the cruise control, just waiting to finish out the last lap…marriage, grandkids, and huge Christmas dinners filled with all of us.

But like all great road trips, life has surprises, and sometimes there is this thing called…

The detour

Oh, the detour! The fork in the road you never saw coming. The unplanned route. The old, bumpy, rutty road that challenges every single decision you ever made and is such a surprise you don't have words. The moment when the pain of this earth collides with the love of heaven, leaving you to question if everything you've always believed is true.

A detour is not a normal twist and turn. It's more than that. It's deeper than wanting your kid to attend a certain college, but they chose a different one. The detour isn't a change in plans, it's a change of direction—a U-turn that spins you around faster than a speeding car hitting a patch of winter's black ice. The road that was clearly laid out before you is nowhere to be found, and you are on a different path—an unmarked trail that leads into the dark unknown.

NO ONE TELLS YOU ABOUT THE DETOUR.

Parenting books are silent on the topic, so you certainly can't plan for it. There's no mention of what to do if your child gets addicted to meth or goes to jail or an unexpected pregnancy happens. There are no bonus chapters at the end that cover the unexpected parts of this journey.

At church, babies are dedicated in front of the church where young parents promise to raise their kids in the ways of the Lord. We join with other parents who are on this same path. We declare Jeremiah 29:11—the promise of a hope and a future—over our kids and believe this verse is about their lives and how amazing things are going to turn out.

What no one ever mentions is that children will develop a mind of their own (you know, that free will thing). Jeremiah 29:11 is not about high school graduations. There is an actual enemy after our kids. An enemy that comes for one purpose and one purpose only…

To steal.

To kill.

And to destroy.

A real enemy, causing real pain, breaking up real families.

You can plan on many unexpected things when you become a parent. You may discover that the straight-A student you thought you would raise, is more like a solid C student. You might find a high school tuba player sitting at your dinner table instead of the sports star you dreamed of. Or you may realize the frilly dresses you bought for your daughter have been exchanged for soccer cleats.

These are all normal things, and learning to watch your kids explore the things they love and become who God made them to be is so exciting, even when they choose a path different from what you envisioned. You leave room for the unexpected, but never expect the biggest change of all—the one that will knock the very breath out of you.

No one talks about an unexpected phone call—one that rocks your world. A conversation containing three words making zero sense…

"Mom, I'm transgender."

Wait, what?

Three words. Three words that I never would have imagined would ever be written into my family's story suddenly took over my life.

What does *transgender* even mean? How was this going to change my family? So many unanswered questions.

Three words transferred me from sleeping to not sleeping, from joy to despair, from happiness to unbearable pain. Those words instilled a fear in me I had never known. A fear for the life of my child…and the very eternal life of my child.

That one phone call changed everything.

In a matter of minutes, every dream I had evaporated. What I envisioned was no more. If my life were a glass vase, this call would have sent it plummeting from a ten-story building, shattering on the pavement below—glass shards scattering so far I could never hope to gather them, much less piece them back together.

Life just stamped my passport with a stop in the LGBTQ community. Surely this was a mistake. There was no way the

Lord would have me face this. Those words are meant for other families. Not ones with praying, Bible-believing parents.

Maybe your family has heard these words too. Maybe you've heard, "Mom, I'm gay." Perhaps you sat in a courtroom, listening to a judge read charges leveled against your child. Maybe you, too, are confused, scared, and wondering how God could ever use this for good. Or perhaps you have clung to Jeremiah 29:11 praying for that hope and a future, but fearing now you won't see either. Now you wonder if that means God's Word is untrue, questioning whether God is still good and if He can fix this?

This is not the book I envisioned people reading about my family. I wanted to author a book about raising the perfect kids and leading a life that turned out even better than those fairy tales I read as a kid. But if I have learned anything in the years since that phone call, it is that I never really was the author of my story.

The control I thought I had was a big lie. God is the one with the pen. He is author of our lives and our kids' lives. The outcome is His and His alone, but in the process of writing that book, He invites us to cling to Him and trust Him. He invites us into His story…the one that does not involve plot twists because He knows the end from the beginning.

That day, as I hung up the phone, I clearly heard these words from the Lord: *"It is your job to love your child; it is My job to save him. Write the truths I tell you each day. You will need them in the days to come. You will need to share them with others. I am with you, and together we will get through this."*

How true that was. In the days following that announcement, I wrote down every thought. Every time I was scared, I would write. Every time my breath wouldn't come, and the tears wouldn't stop, I'd write. Somehow, in this crazy time, the voice of the Lord became clearer than it had ever been before.

Maybe it was because before that phone call, my conversations with Him involved me telling God what I wanted for my family's future. I was consumed with making sure we looked perfect on the outside, never stopping to ask for His plan. Communication was one-sided. I pretty much had my wish list typed up. All I needed was His signature.

The day my dreams shattered, the light of heaven shone brighter than ever. Looking back, I know none of the written words were mine, they all came from the Lord. He knew His words would comfort a grieving mom's heart as she faced the Goliath coming against her family.

Even though I did not know if Goliath would fall, I put my trust in the same One that David the shepherd boy did all those years ago. The God of Israel. The One who knows all. The One the wind and waves obey. The Alpha and Omega. The Beginning and The End. The One who is bigger than any of the letters in the LGBTQ alphabet.

The journal entry I often revisit feels like a prophetic declaration of the path God would lead me on as this story unfolded. Forty-eight hours after that phone call, I wrote in my journal…

The Devil comes to kill, steal, and destroy. He is trying to steal my peace, kill my children, and destroy my future. He will not succeed. HE. WILL. NOT. SUCCEED.

Satan might think he's won, but this battle is just beginning. This fight isn't against flesh and blood, but against Satan and his demons coming straight from hell.

Demons that call our children out from their place at God's table and throw them into the darkness, far from the Light.

Yet, I believe. I believe that even though I do not understand, God has a plan and a purpose to use this. Get ready, Satan…you are in for a ride. You can go straight to hell because you LOSE…I have read the end of the book!

This is my BATTLE CRY...LOVE GOES TO WAR!

That journal entry was the beginning. The start of the fight for my children. A battle waged for their very souls.

I did not know at that point what the war would look like, but that day I decided...*grace will win!* And even though I have no idea how this will all work out, I know, I know, I know...God will win, and the prodigals are coming home. I do not know when. I do not know how. I wish I could tell you to turn right now to the last page of this book so you would see God's victory. But the victory I'm believing in hasn't been written, and yet I know that victory belongs to God, and I have faith, even when I am in the middle parts, and I just cannot see.

While there is no real fairytale book that lets us get a glimpse of our happy endings, there is one Book that is real, and it clearly spells out how this all ends.

We can rest knowing God's Word clearly states He wins in the end. Satan's days are numbered, and they are quickly running out. Revelation 20:10 tells us, "And the devil who had deceived them was thrown into the lake of fire and sulfur where the beast and the false prophet were, and they will be tormented day and night forever and ever."

Read that again. Forever and ever. God wins. He will defeat the enemy once and for all, and I believe with all my heart that on that day, the front row will be reserved for mothers of prodigals where we can witness Satan defeated once and for all.

Until then, the war has started.

PRAYER

Lord, I thank You for Your Word that promises one day You will wipe away every tear. We lay our children at Your feet, trusting You to work all things out for Your glory and their good. Even in the unknown, even in the hard places, I trust in You.

Remind me, Lord, that my happily-ever-after isn't something for this earth, but it's the promise that heaven is coming, and someday the pain of this world will be a distant memory. When I start to doubt and question, show me how to remain close to You. Blind my eyes from obstacles that would cause me any unbelief. Let me see Your hand every day, in all I do.

I lay my dreams, my hopes, and my future down at the foot of the cross. Hold me, Lord, as the unknown brings fear, and let Your perfect peace flow over me each day. My eyes are on You. In Jesus name.

2. OFF-ROADING

THE FIRST FEW SLEEPLESS NIGHTS proved one thing to me—my life had been on autopilot. I just didn't realize it.

For years, I lived in a state of perceived control. I set my parenting GPS and cruised right along. My motto could have been the old commercial slogan, "Set it and forget it."

I assumed I had authority over so many areas of my life. Of course, the *big ones* I knew the Lord oversaw…salvation, money, etc.…but the day-to-day stuff? I had that.

Of course, I had no idea life was about to throw me off the main highway and onto some really rough off-road terrain.

Flying is one of my biggest fears. I'll do anything not to get on a plane. I will literally drive across the country even if it means it will take me way longer to get there. Will the extra driving time cut into my fun time when I arrive at my destination? Of course, but I don't care! I need to have some sort of control in arriving safely.

Because of this crazy fear, I've driven a lot of miles. I set my GPS, fill up the car, and take off. I know the plan before I get started and know exactly how long it's going to take me to arrive. GPS tells me the most direct route, and I trust this little magical friend to guide me.

But sometimes the planned route brings me to an orange

sign with a big arrow that says *Detour,* and as if on cue, my GPS announces, "recalculating."

"I don't have time for a detour," I sigh. Not only will it slow me down, but it also makes me go into unknown territory… places I have never been.

It's a tad scary following a detour. It requires giving control over to the geniuses behind the GPS and trust they know an alternative route that really will get me there safely.

The phone call made me do pretty much the same thing. It required me to release my grip on the parenting steering wheel and allow God to drive the car. My control was an illusion. I now know God leads me and guides me. It is the choices I make in that process that may alter my route.

I have to admit, through the years the parenting process became so familiar to me that I'd sometimes turn off the GPS. Day after day was typical and predictable. At times, praying for the children became words without authority. I just went through the motions. There was nothing to worry about because we were like every other family…and nothing bad happens to Christian families.

The Lord revealed my mistake one afternoon on a road trip to visit my daughter at college a few hours away. I didn't bother to set the GPS. I knew the way. I'd been on the road before.

I set out on my trip and did just fine for a while, but eventually, I made a wrong turn. In my defense, the numbers were similar, and it was a mistake anyone could make…69…65…the numbers were close! I knew the road had a 6 in it!

My mistake took me on an adventure I hadn't planned.

After driving for a while, nothing looked familiar. I pulled over to look at the map and check with my GPS. Sure enough, it wanted me to go somewhere I had never been before. What should have been a two hour drive, turned into four. The recalculation took me through every small town and gravel road in Central Indiana. I had gotten myself in a mess, thinking I could do this all on my own.

And there you have it…the Lord revealed my parenting style and why I was so lost.

I know I am not alone. We all start off on this parenting superhighway in pretty much the same way. We read the books, check the tires for air, fill up our tanks, and begin the journey when we bring those babies home. Months and years go by, and our lives get set on cruise control.

Then it happens. A deer jumps out (or maybe your kid comes out), and your life spins out of control.

When you open your eyes, you find yourself off-roading. There is no map to guide you. GPS can't help. Darkness has replaced the bright lights of the well-lit road. You remind yourself to breathe. There is nothing fun about this unmarked journey. Turning around isn't an option, so you press on.

The parenting detour I was on was scary and dark. I knew no one else on this path. I felt very alone, with no roadmap to guide me. I had to rely on a different kind of GPS…the One that lives inside of me. If I was going to survive the days, weeks, and months to come, walking in a new family dynamic, I would need the Holy Spirit each second of every day.

I thought the Spirit *had been* guiding me before. The truth was, He had been trying, but I wasn't completely listening. It's painful to admit that.

Sure, I prayed and trusted, knowing God had my kids, but I still thought I had some sort of influence over how their lives would turn out.

In reality, I was off-roading in a car without four-wheel drive! To survive, I needed to totally surrender my dreams for my kids…to come to a place where I handed them to my heavenly Father. Not lead and pray later.

Finally, I got on my knees.

"Here they are, Lord," I prayed. "They're Yours. I know You love my kids more than I do, and I trust what You are doing in my family. Lead me. I trust in You and Your plan."

That may be where you've found yourself. Perhaps your parenting journey took a detour, and you don't know how to find any road that looks remotely familiar. I get it. He gets it, and He longs for you to take His hand and follow where He leads, trusting the outcome to Him.

It's not easy and it's something I continue to struggle with. If it were easy, we wouldn't have so many self-help books, and I could end this book by saying, "Life is hard, trust God," and that would be it.

But the truth is, faith looks easy when you don't need it, but it doesn't operate in the good times; it merely exists. Faith is activated when we get bogged down in the trenches of living in a fallen world, fighting an enemy that comes only to steal, kill, and destroy.

Faith and prayer demand action behind them. It requires us to hand our kids back to the One who knew them in the womb.

Psalm 139:13–16 says, "For you formed my inward parts; you knitted me together in my mother's womb. I praise you, for I am fearfully and wonderfully made. Wonderful are your works; my soul knows it very well. My frame was not hidden from you, when I was being made in secret, intricately woven in the depths of the earth. Your eyes saw my unformed substance; in your book were written, every one of them, the days that were formed for me, when as yet there was none of them."

He knows our children. He gave them to us. He knit them together. He knows the number of their days. There is nothing hidden. There are no surprises. There are no detours He doesn't know about.

Nothing is new to God.

But the whole thing was completely new to me.

God was teaching me how much He loved my kids and that I needed to learn to trust Him. This trust required me to give up my motherly grip and run straight to the arms of my Savior to hold me and guide me as I trusted Him and His plan.

It hardly seems right. God gives us a child and we take care of them, keeping them safe every day. Then one day, something happens, and we have to hand them back to the Lord to watch over.

It went against every parenting instinct I had. I didn't know how to give my kids to the Lord and honestly trust Him with their lives. What does that even look like? How do I even get to that point? I needed answers to these questions and a thousand more. I was so far off the known path that just breathing each day was hard work.

Every day my prayers were filled with pleas for God to help me keep my eyes on Him. There were just so many distractions—fear, shame, loss, anger, hate, jealousy—so many ugly things I didn't know my heart contained.

The Lord asked me to confront theology I had learned… jokes I had made…lies I believed. I was in the Refiner's fire, and He was burning away all things that were not of Him.

Yet, this journey also uncovered something new in me…a deep hope. One that believes for the impossible. A faith strong enough to see past anything I witnessed in the natural and believed the truth found in God's supernatural.

I was a work in progress. Surrender did not come easy for me but, I was determined to become someone God could use.

Some days, I easily surrendered my pain. Others, I held it tight like a blanket wrapping me in grief, regret, loneliness, and shame. Nearly every day I told God He picked the wrong person, the wrong family, to wrestle through this mess. How could He possibly make this into something for His glory?

Could beauty come from my heaping pile of pain and loss?

My daily wrestling sessions with God felt like Olympic training drills. Yet, each day, He was faithful—teaching me, building on the day before and laying out the foundation that would guide my life.

FIGHTING FOR THE PRODIGALS AND TRUSTING GOD IN ALL THINGS.

One particularly difficult day, I heard the Lord tell me to take a walk in a nearby park. Our long winter was ending, and it was finally nice enough to venture out for some fresh air.

I bundled up and headed out. The early spring morning was so crisp and clear. Birds chirped and so many other signs of life were reappearing after a great white northern winter.

As I walked around the park, I noticed the biggest, most beautiful bird nest in a nearby tree. I stopped and looked at that nest for a long time, noticing how big it was, where it was in the tree, and how beautiful the dark sticks were against the light sky.

Why had I never noticed it before? I walked this path all the time, but had never noticed it until the leaves were all gone. That nest wasn't visible in the summer or fall. Only the dead of winter revealed what was hidden.

As I stood staring at this nest, I heard the Lord say, "This is what I'm doing to you. I am stripping away everything that is dead, so your beauty can be revealed."

Tears ran down my face. The God of the universe loves me enough to speak to me and mold me into something beautiful He can use. Had the vibrant orange, red, and yellow leaves not dried and fallen off, the beauty of the nest would not have been revealed. If I am not willing to let go of things that are dead and holding me back—like bitterness, hurt, jealousy, shame, and all the other ugly things hidden in my heart—then the beauty within my story will never be seen. My heavenly Father reminded me that day, He was there to walk with me in my pain.

God loves us and never will leave us nor forsake us. There will be good times and troubled times, but He is always there, never leaving us to walk through our disappointments alone. All we need to do is cling to him. Jeremiah 29:13, says, "You will seek me and find me, when you seek me with all your heart."

God was taking my life on a detour—a detour that made me believe I was lost, and that it would kill me. But He was making something beautiful out of it.

Being the parent of a prodigal would not bury me; it was building me into what God wanted me to become. My child was transgender, but I was the one who would be transformed. If I wanted Mercy to call my child's name, I had to allow Mercy to change my heart first. I had to believe God was the God of all the mountains I would face, and that He would provide the equipment to conquer each one.

GOING THROUGH IT...WITH HIM

I love the book *Going on a Bear Hunt*. It's so full of adventure. Each time an obstacle appears, the characters must decide how they will proceed. The best line in the entire book is "You can't go over it. You can't go under it. Oh, no! We've got to go through it."

The Lord was calling me to go through this, but I would not be alone. He was inviting me to follow His lead and lean into Him in the peaceful places, the hard places, and everywhere in between. The journey of my life hadn't ended. It was beginning, and I was certain the future would be bright.

I made three promises to myself in those early days. I promised to never stop believing God was bigger than anything I would face. I promised if I ever found a way out of the pain, I would talk about what I was going through, sharing so other moms wouldn't think they were alone. And finally, I promised to find a community of moms like me, broken and afraid, to go through life with, leaning on one another for support. God has been faithful to answer each of those promises.

I eventually made it to the college to see my daughter that day. My car didn't break down in the middle of a cornfield with no cell phone service. I didn't run out of gas. None of my other fears came true either. In fact, my off-road adventure helped me discover some beautiful old churches that I would love to photograph some day, and countless junk stores to explore.

My attitude went from fear to anticipation, and I knew then that my journey on this new path would lead to beautiful things. The Lord told me not to worry; He promised to be with me and never leave me or forsake me. After the storm a beautiful rainbow would be waiting and I was ready for it.

The best was yet to come.

PRAYER

Lord, thank You for the adventure called life. Thank You for roads that are known, where we can cling to what we know, and thank You for the roads I don't know…for in those, unexpected beauty is found. Thank You, Father, for allowing us to get to know You in ways we wouldn't choose and for leading us on a new path… it is for our good!

This road of parenthood has changed and includes a detour I didn't see coming. Help me trust that I am on the right road and You are leading me. Allow me to see the beauty at every stop on this adventure. Remind me that You are in all places, the ones I planned for and the ones I didn't. Your Word says if I trust in You with all my heart and not lean on my own understanding, that You will make my paths straight. I trust You Father. In all ways. In Jesus name.

3. BEHIND ENEMY LINES

"I FEEL LIKE I'VE BEEN DROPPED behind enemy lines."

It feels odd reading those words, but it is exactly what I felt as I journaled in the days following that life-changing phone call. In those first few days and months, I didn't know what to think anymore and wrestled continuously with my thoughts.

I didn't know what was happening to me, but I knew the Lord was at work. He was uprooting every single preconceived concept I had about whom He loved and for whom He died. He was teaching me so much. All I could do was pray my heart would be receptive to what He was saying, and my mouth would speak His truth to whomever would listen.

One of the first things I had to address were my preconceived ideas. Where did these beliefs come from? Were they biblical truth or something I made up?

I had to ask myself things like where did I get the picture of what God's love looks like? What is my family supposed to look like? I even had to reimagine what heaven might look like and who would be there.

One thing these questions had in common was perfection. God is perfect and if I followed him, I thought I would have a perfect family and we would all end up in a perfect heaven.

The picture I created in a Pinterest-perfect world was nowhere near what was happening in my family. So, if I had been striving for picture-perfect perfection and had ended up here, I had to assume I had failed and that God's love had limits. I found that incredibly disappointing.

The Bible is full of stories with disappointments. One of the first ones that comes to mind is of Joseph and Mary. Talk about life taking a turn. They had a plan. They were engaged and intended to get married and have their happily ever after. But there was this one minor problem—an unplanned pregnancy.

Every one of Joseph's dreams must have crumbled with that announcement. So, he drafted a way to clean the mess up, say goodbye, and exit the scene quietly. The decisions were made in his heart, but the Lord had other ideas.

An angel showed up to declare God's plan, and promised it all would be okay. Matthew 1:20 replays this account in what was to be a huge life detour and yet was the right road to take.

I can't help but think Joseph asked God the same questions I was asking. "I follow the Law; how could this happen to us? What are people going to say? But this isn't what a normal God-fearing family looks like. Why does this have to happen this way?"

The answer, as the angel announced, was simple: *Do not be afraid*. Joseph's disappointment mirrored my own. But because he laid down his dreams at God's altar, I can call myself a child of God 2,000 years later.

I could almost hear the Lord telling me to lay down the idea of my ideal family and "Do not be afraid."

The problem I had wasn't from the situation; it was from the picture I had for my family. I had pre-planned what it was to look like. It was like getting a puzzle and putting it together by following the picture on the box. A picture I made. I should know where every piece would go. The problem now was I had the pieces, but God had erased the image on the box.

The Spirit reminded me to let go of the picture of what my family should look like. Instead, He would lead me into a deeper understanding of who He was and who I was in Him.

He had the final picture of my family and my life, and it was going to be beautiful. So much more glorious than I could ever imagine. I simply needed to take one piece out of the box at a time and let Him show me where it fit. He didn't want to build a picture, but my purpose. This was going to be challenging. I had to believe it was all God, even if it didn't feel good.

WHO CAN I LOVE?

Growing up in a conservative church, I had a clear understanding of groups I could love and who were off-limits. Anyone with an alphabet letter attached to their identity topped that list.

Many Christians quote verses to back up their understanding of God's hate for these people. And as an evangelical Christian, I was expected to join my fellow brothers and sisters in condemning them all.

It seemed easy enough…until one day someone I loved joined the group.

I had so many questions. What am I supposed to do? Am I allowed to love my child? Does the church accept and love them? Does God? Who will help me figure out this path?

I have always prayed, "Here I am Lord, send me. Let me be your hands and feet." But what I meant was, "Here I am Lord, send me to the loveable. Send me to the popular. Send me on the shiny, sparkly ministries. I don't want to be in the trenches with the real sinners. I'm more comfortable with sinners like me…the ones people like. Send me there so I won't get dirty or smelly."

The Lord knows I have said I *never* want to go *there*…so why would He send me there? I'm convinced the Hebrew meaning of the word *never* must be *report to work tomorrow*.

My prayers are different now. I don't have answers, but if my pain and situation can help someone else so they don't feel alone, then so be it. My prayer is that all anyone sees in me is Jesus…His grace and His love, His ability to make the unworthy worthy, the unclean clean, and the outcast accepted.

I was now fighting not just for the one I love, but for the ones God loves.

I wrestled with these questions for a long time. About a week after that call, someone asked me to help in the nursery at a daycare for a few days. While rocking a sweet little one, tears flooded my eyes as I thought of my own sweet baby. The baby I rocked and held and sang to and promised to never stop loving.

Never. Nothing could ever make me stop loving my child. Not anything they say, do, or want to become. The Lord whispered that was the exact thing He wanted to hear me say. He wasn't asking me to quit loving my child. He wanted me to let Him love my child more. He was reminding me that my heart was walking around outside of my chest in each of my kids and I couldn't turn that love off if I wanted to. Love is what a mom is about, and I wanted to stay right there.

But true love comes with surrender. I had to let God work. I needed to listen to Him instead of what the church said. God wanted me to study His Word and ask what He thought of His children. This lesson would take me on one wild ride. Nothing was going to be normal anymore, and I couldn't float around in a boat learning about God's ways this time. He was asking me to get out of the boat and step into some very deep water, all while keeping my eyes on Him.

SIN ON DISPLAY

Since I worked in children and youth ministry, I occasionally took the kids on little fun outings. One summer, we spent a day at a local amusement park. As we walked past the usual row of games, a worker called out, inviting people to step on a giant scale so he could guess their weight.

Who in their right mind would hop on a scale at an amusement park and let everyone watch as the game attendant, microphone in hand, announced their weight to the world? How could anyone willingly put themselves on display like that? What if he guessed twenty pounds too high? There is no way I would I broadcast my cupcake addiction to the universe!

As I sat and giggled at the thought of getting on that scale in public, the Lord whispered in my ear. Everyone has struggles. Everyone has addictions, hidden secrets…thoughts they hide.

Most of the time, those struggles are inside. No one knows about them. They are tucked neatly away, hidden from sight. However, not everyone can hide the things they struggle with. They are on display for the world to see, judge, and laugh at.

That is exactly what my child and others like him go through. It must feel so awkward knowing the entire world knows what you struggle with. I can't even imagine my deepest struggle being announced on a Sunday morning in church. The stares, the judgments…it would all be so awful. I'm not sure I'd ever go back.

As I pondered this revelation, I prayed and meditated on Scriptures about who Jesus literally died for…sinners. What did He think of them? Why does the church seem to focus so much on outward disobedience and not on inward hidden sin? Why are the alphabet letters placed so high on the sin scale? Was that the only abomination to God? I sat down and really studied the Bible and found Proverbs 6:16–19.

"There are six things that the LORD hates, seven that are an abomination to him: haughty eyes, a lying tongue, and hands that shed innocent blood, a heart that devises wicked plans, feet that make haste to run to evil, a false witness who breathes out lies, and one who sows discord among brothers."

I realized many of my sins were on that list. The NIV Bible calls them detestable…*detestable*…to the Lord. I had only heard the word *detestable* applied to sins of a certain group. I never thought my hidden sins were detestable to God. But there is no ranking of sin, despite what my church taught me. My sin was just as ugly. The disobedience in my life broke my Father's heart as much as the outward sins of others.

EATING WITH SINNERS

Jesus had one mission. To seek and save the lost. I love the story of Jesus eating with sinners and how the religious people reacted.

"And as he reclined at table in his [Levi] house, many tax collectors and sinners were reclining with Jesus and his disciples, for there were many who followed him. And the scribes of the Pharisees, when they saw that he was eating with sinners and tax collectors, said to his disciples, 'Why does he eat with tax collectors and sinners?' And when Jesus heard it, he said to them, 'Those who are well have no need of a physician, but those who are sick. I came not to call the righteous, but sinners'" (Mark 2:15–17).

He came to be a place where the sick can get help. He came to save them, heal them, and love them. So why is it so hard for us who don't struggle, to allow those who do to have access to Jesus? Why was this so radical to the Pharisees?

The answer can be found when you take a deeper look at the temple in the Old Testament.

The high priest, who was from the Levitical line, had to go to great lengths to appear before a holy God. He was the only one who had access to the Holy of Holies, where God's presence resided, and he was allowed into this sacred place only once a year. God gave Moses the instructions on how the priests were to clean and purify themselves before entering. We can read this in Exodus 30:17–20.

"The LORD said to Moses, 'You shall also make a basin of bronze, with its stand of bronze, for washing. You shall put it between the tent of meeting and the altar, and you shall put water in it, with which Aaron and his sons shall wash their hands and their feet. When they go into the tent of meeting, or when they come near the altar to minister, to burn a food offering to the Lord, they shall wash with water, so that they may not die.'"

According to the Mishnah, a written collection of Jewish oral traditions, the high priest had to immerse himself five times and wash his hands and feet ten times. This purification process is symbolic of spiritual cleansing and preparation for encountering the divine presence of a holy God.

Then, they literally tied a rope around his leg before he went in, so if he died they could pull him out. Today, we walk right into our churches on Sunday morning, grab our lattes, and nonchalantly walk into the sanctuary...never once thinking about the fact that we are entering His holy presence.

The cleansing process later grew into the Jewish leaders requiring *all* people, whether from the Levitical line or not, to enter ritual baths before entering the Temple Mount. Archaeologists have unearthed more than one hundred baths surrounding the modern-day Temple Mount complex. So, Jewish leaders traded in God's basin of bronze for baths big enough for everyone to fully immerse in before entering the holy places of God.

When Jesus came on the scene, the Pharisees couldn't fathom why He would teach, let alone sit and eat with, the outcasts of society. Jewish law required the total cleansing before going to God, but Jesus allowed sinners in His presence, knowing He was the one providing the cleansing. The leaders of the Law just couldn't get it.

Today, many believers make the same mistake. They label, call out, and cast aside the ones Jesus came to save. Sinners are led to believe they have to clean themselves up before coming to God. We ask them to bathe in the ritual bath of religion before they enter the saving grace of Jesus.

The Pharisees were wrong and so are our expectations. As disciples of Jesus we are called to minister to the lost. We have to adopt a "we catch them, He cleans them" policy. Jesus said He would make us fishers of men. He never called us to clean fish!

THERE IS NO DIFFERENCE

There's no difference between the outward sins of a lost soul and those we hide within. We have to stop caring about *their sin verses our sin* and determining whose sin is worse.

Instead, let's see people—especially those we love—as Jesus sees them. As sinners He loves.…whom he died for…who are lost (as we once were) and not yet found.

We need to change trite remarks like "hate the sin, love the sinner" into "thankful I've been forgiven, and I won't stop praying till blind eyes are opened."

Romans 2:4 says the kindness of God leads us to repentance. We need to remember that! Comedian Mark Lowry once said, "Love the sinner, hate the sin? How about: Love the sinner, hate your own sin! I don't have time to hate your sin. There are too many of you! Hating my sin is a full-time job. How about you hate your sin? I will hate my sin and let's just love each other!"

For me, hating my sin is it's own full-time job! I need to work on myself before I can point out someone else's flaws.

Is this a free pass to just ignore sin? Absolutely not! It is prioritizing self-examination over the condemnation of others.

Jesus said in Matthew 7:3–5, "Why do you see the speck that is in your brother's eye, but do not notice the log that is in your own eye? Or how can you say to your brother, 'Let me take the speck out of your eye,' when there is the log in your own eye? You hypocrite, first take the log out of your own eye, and then you will see clearly to take the speck out of your brother's eye.'"

Jesus was teaching us to examine our own lives and hearts, and know what is in them, before we start judging others.

To judge is to speak a conclusion on a matter. Jesus said that is not our job. We are to examine our own hearts and remember who we were before the Holy Spirit called us to repentance. When we see our sin as filthy rags before the Lord, and remove that plank, we'll be able to see the lost the way the Lord sees them…compassionately, not as lost causes but lost children not yet home. It will lead us to pray without ceasing, believing the Way Maker will make a way to bring His children home.

My new parenting journey was before me, and I knew what direction the Lord was calling me to go. I was scared. I am still scared. It is the hardest thing the Lord has asked me to do, but I refuse to let my fear cripple me.

Instead, my fear has become my fuel to move forward, trusting God each step of the way! The path before me was to surrender my children to the Lord's care. It didn't matter what anyone thought or how fearful I was moving forward…I knew fighting for the lost was who I now was. Jesus never loved sinners from a distance. He never loved me from a distance. The blood of Jesus connected the darkest places of our hearts to the Light that came to save.

The Pharisees' spirit is alive today. Religion tells us Christ's love is like a brake…putting stops and limits on the way we love.

That is wrong. God's love is an accelerator. It is all gas, no brakes. He pursued the worst of the worst—the outcasts and unlovable. He pursued me and He pursued you. He is calling all of us in this hour to open our hearts and our tables to the ones He died for and allow them at the feet of a Savior who can change them.

My life was changing. I was becoming who God was calling me to be. I now knew how awful a sinner I was before I came to the saving knowledge of Jesus Christ and how He was walking me, step by step, in loving all His children. The journey was just beginning. The road would be hard, but I was thankful the plank in my eye was being removed and I was seeing more clearly each day.

PRAYER

Lord, thank You for loving us enough to call us to repentance. Thank You for never leaving us in our sin, but You reach us through whatever it takes. Your love for us will not stop. Thank You, Lord, for pursuing me at my worst. When necessary, remind me how wretched a sinner I was before coming to the redeeming grace of Jesus. Thank You for challenging my every thought and continue to open my eyes to Your vast love…a love that cannot be measured. May my eyes of compassion open wider each day. Continue to break my heart for the things that break Yours. In Jesus name.

4. WHERE DID I GO WRONG?

I LOVE THE TIME OF YEAR when the heat of summer gives way to cool fall nights. I hate to end those lazy days by the pool, but I am eager to pull out my favorite sweatshirts and trade my lemonade for hot chocolate.

A few weeks into September last year, I brought in my beautiful hibiscus plants. It was my first time trying my hand at growing these beauties. Strategically placed around the pool, they brought me endless joy with the big, beautiful flowers. I bought them specifically because they had a promise attached to them…that they would bloom all winter if I put them in a sunny spot and took care of them…a promise I needed based on my gardening history.

This was not the first time I had tried to nurture summer plants all winter. There were fig trees in 2019. They died, but I decided it was not my fault. It must be the wrong region for figs. Then there was the lemon tree of 2020. It did so well all summer and had three of the most adorable baby lemons growing when I brought it in. I could almost taste the fresh lemonade I would have. However, it, too, did not survive. I blame its death on the fact that it got too cold by the window.

However, things were going to be different this year. My beautiful hibiscus plants were going to thrive. I was going to enjoy their blooms all winter. They had a promise!

As the days grew colder, I noticed those completely healthy plants I had taken care of for months were anything but healthy. Each day more leaves fell to the ground. It would be okay, I told myself. Losing a few leaves is like losing a few pounds. We all need to do it. Besides, these plants came with a promise that they would thrive all winter.

Eventually, I emailed the company some pictures looking for reassurance. "It's going to be okay," they told me. "Just keep watering, feeding, and keep them in a warm spot."

One morning, I discovered all the leaves had fallen. My beautiful plants were now dead sticks poking out of the dirt. I could hardly remember what they looked like just months ago. The beautiful flowers from all summer, gone. Hopes of having beautiful blooms all winter, gone. The dreams of successfully keeping my plants alive for an entire year, gone.

As I bent to pick up the leaves, tears fell. I was a horrible gardener. Why do they always die when I try so hard and follow all the rules. I did everything I could, but it wasn't enough. Why is it never enough?

The rush of tears made me realize my mind had shifted from plants to my family. I was no longer grieving over my dead plants; I was grieving over my dead dreams and sobbing questions to God about my parenting.

Why can't I be a better mom? Why did my kids walk away from the Lord? How did this happen? Where did I go wrong? How can You still love me when I let You down with the one job You gave me…to point my children to You? God, I failed! Oh, how You must hate me!

The tears continued as I reviewed everything I did as a parent. I could check all the boxes. Church…check. Christian school…check. Youth group, youth camp, praise bands… check, check, check. I did everything right. Why did my kids walk away? I just don't understand.

Dead plants didn't cause my meltdown that day…a heavy burden of prodigal children did. In my mind, gardening was just one more thing I failed. Not only did I have a promise from the plant people it would be okay, I felt I had a promise from God that having kids who serve the Lord was also guaranteed.

Verses quoted for years in Christian circles, promised me it would all be okay. I tattooed those verses as truth on my heart, not once wondering if I interpreted them correctly. The two biggest ones were…

"Train up a child in the way he should go; even when he is old he will not depart from it" (Proverbs 22:6), and Jeremiah 29:11, "For I know the plans I have for you, declares the LORD, plans for welfare and not for evil, to give you a future and a hope."

I blindly believed everyone else's interpretations of these verses. I was convinced they were written for me and my parenting journey. "I cannot mess up this parenting thing…no way," I reasoned. "And, if I do, the kids will come back! It's what the Word says."

SO, WHAT HAPPENED?

I am 100 percent sure God's Word is true, and He has given *every single word* of it to guide us in our lives in any scenario that comes up. We are talking about the inspired Word of God, so it *is* the truth, but is it an all-out, drop-the-mic guarantee I do not have to worry-about-my-parenting kind of truth? Does it mean what I *hope* it means? That it will all be okay?

I needed to figure out how these verses applied to my family and our future based on what I was now seeing with my eyes and what the Scripture was saying. I had to know what these verses meant and how I could claim them and apply them to my family. And to do that, I had to dig deep into the difference between a biblical principal and a biblical promise.

THE PROMISE?

I approached Proverbs 22:6 with a heart that needed answers. I studied. I read. And I looked up each word of this verse in the original language. I needed to know the meaning and if I could sleep at night knowing there was nothing to worry about. I had three overarching questions.

1. Are my works attached to this truth?
2. If kids leave, do they always return?
3. If these things don't happen, does that make God's Word untrue?

To answer these questions, we must find out what a proverb really is and what it is not. *Merriam-Webster* defines a proverb as a "collection of moral sayings and counsels forming a book of canonical Jewish and Christian Scripture." The book of Proverbs falls into the genre of wisdom literature.

Proverbs include wise sayings for one to follow. God gave them to us as guides. They are general truths about life, not blanket promises from God that will come true in every parenting situation you will encounter.

A wise saying is different from biblical truth, and biblical truth is different from a biblical promise. Biblical truths are principles we, as Christians, endeavor to live by. There are consequences to violating a biblical truth. God has given each of us free will. It says in Deuteronomy 30:19–20, "I call heaven and earth to witness against you today, that I have set before you life and death, blessing and curse. Therefore choose life, that you and your offspring may live, loving the Lord your God, obeying his voice and holding fast to him, for he is your life and length of days, that you may dwell in the land that the Lord swore to your fathers, to Abraham, to Isaac, and to Jacob, to give them."

CHOOSE. WE ALWAYS HAVE A CHOICE.

Ouch. This is not what I wanted to learn.

Have you ever been in a Bible study or sat through a sermon with someone boldly state that raising good kids is easy?

It is usually a mom with kids under the age of five declaring there is no reason kids should wander. After all, it's all about you training them.

The world now includes social media. Daily you could log on and see any popular Christian pastor or singer showing you how they raise their children. Color-coded chore charts, chalkboard walls of prayers, and memorization of the works of Spurgeon for homework each week.

Okay, maybe the last one is a little much, but these videos and parenting blogs always make me laugh. I love that they are bringing their kids up in the Lord. I applaud them for the training they are doing, but for those with prodigals, we know it is not so easy.

I want to tell them to please come back in sixteen years and update us when little Timmy has hung out with the wrong crowd, little Jimmy skipped school yesterday to get high, and you found out little Becky is pregnant at fifteen.

Our hope in biblical principles does not equate to a promise of parenting perfection. There is no magic formula for raising children to love the Lord.

The problem with this way of thinking involves work. Our work. We take our kids to church. We pray with them. We discipline them. We do all the things. We, we, we. We do all the Christian works, but what happens when it isn't enough, and our kids walk away? It makes us question what else is not true.

The gospel is never about our work. It is about Jesus and the finished work He did on the cross. Nothing we do or don't do for ourselves, or the ones we love, can earn their way into heaven.

Parenting is not a gamble. We are not dropping quarters into a slot machine each time we complete a Christian act and hope when it's time to pull the lever and send them into the world that the jackpot comes up. Putting the outcome in the works of our hands causes anger and confusion when the outcome is less than we hoped for.

The grief many parents experience stems from them thinking they did not do enough. The list of woulda, coulda, shoulda guilt is long…

We should have gone to church on Wednesdays.

We should have had more Bible memory.

We should have said longer prayers.

We should have_____ (you fill in the blank).

Pulling one verse out and comparing it to our parenting situation makes us think the things we *didn't* do had greater impact than the things we did.

We cannot place the outcome for eternal salvation on our parenting. Our hope is not lost because we got things wrong. We need to place our hope in what God can do (and is doing) with what we gave. Our weakness is always His gain. We will never be enough, but He is always enough (2 Cor 12:9–11). We must keep our feet on the rock of Jesus Christ and not on the shifting sand of our earthly limitations.

Desperate parents claim the last half of Proverbs 22 as a promise—that no matter what, the kids will come back. But if we're honest, we know it isn't true. There are children every day who won't turn from their sin. All across the nation and around the globe, parents lose their kids. Some will come back, but others don't.

TRAINING VS. DEDICATION

When kids rebel, it shakes us to the core, making us question the very love of God. Does He not love my child? Does He even love me? How could He let this happen?

I had to dig deeper still into what Proverbs 22:6 truly says. If we go back to the original text and look at the Hebrew meaning, we see it isn't a promise based on anything we can do.

Strong's Concordance, 2596, translates "train up" as the Hebrew verb *chânak*. It means to dedicate. Chânak is used five times in the Bible, with four of those times meaning how a dwelling is dedicated. The Old Testament speaks of the temple being chânaked. It meant it was owned by God—and set apart for His purpose.

If a soldier was at war and had not chânaked his home, he was excused so he could go home and dedicate that house and live in it, so no one else could claim ownership.

If you apply this to raising your child and what Proverbs 22:6 is saying, it means there is nothing you as a parent can do, or not do, that will change the outcome of your family.

The promise is not that your child will not stray, the promise is that they belong to the Father, and He will not stray from them.

He claims them. He guides them. And He will never leave them. When we chânak a child in the way he should go, we are letting go and letting God.

The same is true if we assume that Jeremiah 29:11 is a postcard handwritten for our kids to speak over them at every milestone, guiding them throughout life, orchestrating each detail to turn out good. Here is a news flash…

That verse is not about them.

Far removed from high school graduations and baby dedications, scholars agree the prophet Jeremiah gave this message to the Jewish nation before they were led into a seventy-year Babylonian captivity. The future of every one of them was death or slavery. The overarching message was not full of hope, but of judgement for a nation gone astray. Jeremiah was telling them they would not be rescued from this trial. Their captivity was on the horizon. There was no escaping it.

Even knowing this, it is easy to still twist the verse and think "yeah, it was for them, but it still will turn out okay and the future is bright." Again, we must go back to the context of the writing and what the prophet was saying. The Lord laid out His plan to allow trial, but He also assured Jeremiah of His promise, to prosper the nation again one day…in another generation.

It made no promises that the people reading it would all live and survive the coming storm. He didn't promise they would see redemption. The promise was that He was a faithful God and that His hand was on the outcome of the nation, setting them up to one day receive their promised Messiah.

The Western church must get out of the habit of applying Scripture to *me*, and instead apply it to *us. We,* as children of the King, will have a hope and a future as He gathers His church and calls us home. He makes no promises about who will make the rapture, only that if we accept Him, we will go. He has given each of us an invitation to be part of the hope and a future.

We need to allow for our children's return to be based on their free will. It is an individual's choice if they respond to the gospel invitation. God does not assign heaven and hell as a reward or punishment. He leaves the decision to accept His grace up to each individual. Salvation is like an airplane about to crash. When you are born, you are on the airplane. To get off the crashing plane, a parachute is offered. His name is Jesus.

Everyone has the same opportunity for a parachute. As parents, we teach our kids about this parachute. We show them how to put it on. We show them where all the clasps, ropes, and everything that makes that parachute open are located. We go over it time and time again. But we cannot put that parachute on them. They must choose to wear it themselves.

God's love must become heart knowledge, not just head knowledge. We can help them, point them, and urge them, but in the end, not all will put that parachute on.

So, should we despair that we have zero control over the decisions our kids make? Absolutely not! Parents are seed planters. We will continue to put the seeds in our kids. We will continue to point them to Jesus. Every chance we get, we will show them the way to eternity.

God and His words do not return void. All those seeds will never leave. You did not fail in planting those seeds; you just must be patient and water them with your tears as prayers. The only way to come to the cross is if the Holy Spirit draws them. We cannot give up based on what our eyes are seeing. We must stay in faith and believe for more.

God's Word is truth. As parents, it is our job to plant those truths in our children. But the promise isn't that they will not fall. The promise is that the Spirit will continue to draw them until they are home.

The promise we need to focus on is that God loves us…and them. He will not leave us or forsake us…or our children. The promise is not in the answer; the promise is in the trusting. We can put our trust in the Lord and His perfect will with the outcome. Our mistakes do not have to be counted as strikes against our children. We do not have to beat ourselves up over what we missed because the Lord still knows every hair on our children's head (Matthew 10:30).

The promise we hold tightly to is that God is in control, and that promise is fulfilled daily. Psalm 121:4 says, "Behold, he who keeps Israel will neither slumber nor sleep." God sees and knows every move we make. He sees every move our children make. Nothing is hidden.

We did not go wrong in our parenting; we went wrong in our expectations of who is in charge. We must remember that our children were never truly ours. He gave them to us, knowing the exact deposit we would place in their lives. He knows the outcome of those deposits and asks us to trust Him for redemption to come…no matter how long it takes.

The promise of my plants living…yeah…it didn't turn out so well. Winter was not kind to them. Yet, I know that after winter comes the promise of spring. Fresh growth, new leaves, new flowers. What looks dead now might not be dead at all. Fresh growth could sprout. I must keep believing! I must believe in plants, and I must believe in my kids.

God has this.

PRAYER

Lord, thank You for taking my parenting crumbs and making something beautiful out of them. Remind me that when I dedicated my children to You, You promised to never take Your eyes off them. I know You will see them through every battle they face and that nothing is a surprise to You. And I know You love them so much more than I do, and Your promise is for hope and a future. Help me to let go and let Your plan unfold. Remind me of the eternity in heaven that awaits. In Jesus name.

5. EMOTIONS

ONE OF MY FONDEST MEMORIES growing up is of a sleepover at my friend Kendra's house.

We all loaded up in the back of her dad's El Camino and drove down the old highway—at what I now know was way too fast—laughing and screaming, going up and down the hills! Long live the seventies and no laws regarding children riding in the back of an open truck bed with no protection devices, all while ignoring speed limit laws! It was like having our own roller coaster! It is the best memory ever.

Going up and down those hills as a teenager was fun. Now that I'm older, I no longer seek those thrills. I am happy to keep my seatbelt on and safely drive the speed limit.

My new parenting adventure was like that ride in the back of the El Camino—a roller coaster ride of emotions. Up, up, up, down, down, down. It changed daily.

Walking in this truth of having a prodigal has brought every emotion out of me. I have extreme sadness; I have times of great joy watching the Lord work. I also have much fear, loneliness, panic, and doubt. I have fits of anger and at times I am not even sure who I'm most mad at…God, my child, society, or myself.

If you can think of the emotion, I can promise you I have had it. This ride has taken me through many hills and through many valleys, and unlike that slumber party memory, it has not been fun.

I thought I'd gone through every emotion possible, until one day, a new one crept up. This one was deep within me, and it showed up in the most joyous of times—in a baby announcement.

Recently, some special friends shared a great joy they were experiencing. They were going to be grandparents, and not just one baby, but two of their beautiful daughters were pregnant. This family has been special to us since our teenage years. We married and started families at the same time and cheered each other on over the decades. Distance separated us but keeping up with their growing family was easy with social media. I was over the moon happy for them.

During the next few months, it was fun to watch all their anticipation. Double everything. Belly photos, gender reveals, and showers. Joy flowed out of each post. Each time I read something, I always thanked God for this double blessing. I was happy for this beautiful family. All the pictures showed their smiles, always so beautiful and full of anticipation. It was sheer family perfection.

I felt like I was on baby watch with them. I checked every day to see if these double blessings had come yet. When it was time for the babies to be born, the girls had their babies a week apart…just like their parents and us had twenty-eight years earlier. The first pictures of these sweet babies together reminded me of the photos we took of our own beautiful children. The images took me right back to the sweet photo of our own babies, taken decades earlier. My excitement and love for them overflowed.

As I watched these babies grow over the next few months, my excitement and happiness turned into something different.

I found myself not wanting to see more pictures. I stopped looking at any post by anyone that involved their family's happiness. Suddenly I noticed everyone was having grand-babies…*everyone!* There were babies popping up everywhere and joyous families celebrating. It wasn't making me happy for them anymore; it was slowly killing me.

In a moment of extreme pain, I decided to get these updates out of my daily view. I unfollowed every friend on social media. *Everyone.* I didn't want to see happiness from anyone, especially the joy I wanted but was sure I never would have. Those hidden feelings bubbled to the surface, and they were not good. It took me a while to admit to myself what I was feeling.

Jealousy.

I was sincerely happy for them but mixed with that happiness was the knowledge my heart carried—and Satan whispered—this will never be me. The joy I had for this beautiful family shared a space with the jealousy my heart held. Jealousy that screamed that God had forgotten me. Jealousy reminded me my family was very different from other families, and my loss would span generations. The depth of this loss opened the floodgates of tears that had not come out of me for months.

I wasn't trusting God with any of it. I tried to pick apart my emotions so I could see what I was trying to process. I prayed every day and asked God to answer the cries of my heart…to one day become a grandma and if that wasn't possible, to take away the desire I had to become one.

As months went by, so many more of our friends announced babies of their own coming and with each announcement, I felt like another stake was driven into my heart. I was genuinely excited for each family, but oh how I wished one day it would be me. I even had my grandma name picked out. Would I ever get to use it?

Only God knew the answer, and I had to get to a place where I trusted Him and His timing to make it happen. And if it didn't, I had to learn to trust Him with that, too.

It wasn't easy. Surrender never is. I felt like I was being asked to give up every dream I had for my family. Now God was showing me another area I needed to hand over. I squeezed tightly on this one, clinging to my plans for grandchildren. Trusting God would not come easy. My greatest desire was to tell my grandchildren about Jesus. I just couldn't process the thought of not being able to do that someday.

Maybe you, too, have been there. One minute you rejoiced over amazing news, and the next you're consumed with sadness over what you will never have. How could God be in both emotions at the same time? Could joy and sadness share space?

During my prayer time one day, God reminded me of a story in 1 Kings 20. I quickly opened my Bible and turned to the chapter. What I read was a beautiful reminder of the omnipresent God we serve.

The story is about two battles and the sovereignty of God over both. The first battle took place during fall in the hill country. Israel was at war with the Syrians and defeated them. The king of Syria escaped, and his officials advised him why this loss happened. They told him the gods of Israel are gods of the hills, and that's why they were stronger and defeat happened. Verse 23 says, "let us [the Syrians] fight against them in the plain, and surely we will be stronger than they." So, they decided t battle again, this time in a different place where their gods would not be.

Spring came and the two sides met again, this time it took place in the valley because the Syrians thought they could defeat Israel there. They thought God could not be in both places. They were wrong and suffered a mighty defeat that day as well.

They discovered the God of Israel is a God of the hills and the valleys. His sovereign power is not limited to one location or one emotion. He reigns supreme over *every single place* on this earth and *every single place* in our hearts. He is on every hill and every valley. He is at every announcement and every loss.

That was the mistake I made, and many parents of prodigals make. I assumed God can only be a God who meets us in the perfect places. The minute things get hard, I ask God where He is. I don't allow Him to work in my pain because I automatically assume He has left me.

That is a lie. I knew then that God knew my deepest desire to one day be a grandma. He reminded me He was the God of the hills and valleys, the highs and lows, and of gains and losses. He was in every emotion I could feel, and just as He did for the army in 1 Kings, He was fighting my battle and victory would be His.

This journey continued to be about me and my walk with the Lord. He continued to put my every thought in the Refiner's fire and mold me into a vessel He could use for His kingdom. I had to learn to trust His timetable and believe what I prayed for was in God's hands.

I had to give Him my hills and my valleys and really, truly believe the battle was His. I was learning to not worry about earthly things like the titles I hope to one day wear, but to keep my focus on where it belongs...on kingdom business. This road I am on has difficulties, and I knew God was in them all. He was with me on the hills of parenting success, and He was holding me tight in the valley of loss.

If you, like me, have found yourself facing emotions that have been hidden deep within you, emotions you didn't even know you had, I want to encourage you to pour those out before the cross. Speak those emotions aloud. Let God be the God of every hill and valley of your life.

Ask Him to uncover the emotions you have not fully surrendered and let Him flood those areas with His love and rest, knowing the outcome is in His hands. Allow God turn your pain into an opportunity to trust Him more. No matter where you find yourself, on the mountain or in the valley, He is there. His grace is enough, and in both places, you are standing in His love.

PRAYER

Lord, thank You for the mountains in my life. Those times everything worked out and I had parenting wins. I also praise You for those times I fell hard to the valley of pain and loss, and had parenting fails. I know, Lord, You are the God of both places and there isn't a place or an emotion You are not in. Help me to keep my eyes on You and not on earthly titles and timelines, but on my eternal destiny You have ordained before the beginning of time. Let me experience Your love in every place I find myself…the highs, the lows, and every place in between. In Jesus name.

6. KEEPING THE SECRET

I HAVE ALWAYS HAD A SOFT SPOT for other moms.

Anytime I hear of a tragedy, my first thoughts are always of the mama. Each time there is a school shooting, I think of all the moms. The ones whose children were injured and the ones who are the moms of the ones doing the injuring. If I hear of a wreck where teenagers are doing things they should not be and lives are lost, I think of the moms, especially the mom of the driver. I cannot help it. For me, their pain seems the worst.

I think of the guilt that mom must endure. Did she see the warning signs? Can you imagine the shame she must have felt for her child, knowing he or she has caused so much pain. I think of the closeness of her family, gone in an instant. My heart breaks thinking about how alone she must feel. The worst part must be the loss of her hopes and dreams.

We moms, we plan. We dream. We secretly hold our family's future on our shoulders. We dream of grandkids. We store our children's favorite toys so we can one day get them out for their children. We plan for those big Christmas dinners and what it will look like with the kids, grandkids, and all the chaos that comes with sharing a holiday meal. We plan all the places we'll take the grandkids and what our grandparent name will be.

Then, in a moment, it all slips away.

The loss isn't just what people see on the surface. It's deeper. It's your future…your dreams, hopes, and plans. All of it is gone and what's left is replaced with tears and pain and so much uncertainty. What once seemed so easy is now hard. The future is different, and we did not ask for this change.

I don't know the loss of a physical death of a child, but I've experienced the death of the dream of the life I thought my child would live. No one understands. They don't know what to say, so they say nothing.

The loss can also be found as you hold your family's place in a pew on a Sunday morning. The stares and whispers from the Christian crowd pile on shame, making it hard to even hold up your head to find the gaze of Christ. It's becoming okay to be alone and broken in the back row, because no one wants to talk about less than perfect families.

If you are the parent of a prodigal, you know this pain. When there has been a physical death, people show up at your door with casseroles and cards. When your kids turn their backs on God, there are no delivered dinners. There are no cards that say, "Sorry your son became your daughter, that must be weird for you, happy Tuesday!"

It is a hidden, lonely pain that is rarely shared. It's the scarlet letter of Christian parenting.

Less than a month after getting my new title of mother of a transgendered child, I was scheduled to go on a mission trip. I was such a mess of emotions that I originally thought I would cancel my trip and stay home to nurse my pain.

It took took a lot of prayer before I let God speak to my heart about going. I knew I needed this trip. It would be a reminder God is active over this entire world and is in everything everywhere. I needed to get back to the bigger picture of the gospel I was called to proclaim.

I went on that trip and the Lord was there each minute of every day. I hid the blanket of sorrow I wore each day. I stayed focused on the mission and what we needed to do to bring God's love to the people we served.

When it was time to leave, I found myself afraid of going home. Distance had made my new life twist manageable—out of sight, out of mind. But as I sat in the airport, dread washed over me. The unknown of the whole situation was so unsettling. I didn't know how my new life was going to look and what kind of normal I would ever have again.

As I boarded the plane, I asked God to be with me and make Himself known to me in this new life. I thanked Him for the few weeks to clear my brain and the distraction from all I had to learn in this new life. It was time to face it again, but I was thankful for the few hours I had to work out my thoughts.

Or so I thought. As I sat down in my seat, I noticed him—a transgendered flight attendant.

Really, Lord? I can't do this! My new reality was not going to be put on the back burner for a few hours. It was going to be on display for all to see.

I wasn't worried about the flight attendant. It was everyone else on the plane that would make me uncomfortable. I watched for the sneers, the jokes, the glances. I saw them all and my heart hurt so very much for this person.

As our flight ended and we exited the plane, I waited for what I feared was coming—talk about the flight attendant from the others I had worked with. I didn't think they were horrible people. I just didn't want to face what I knew deep down in my heart—the Christian crowd would not be a support to me.

As we all stood around talking and waiting to catch our next flight, it happened. Somehow I managed to hold my tears and my tongue through their jokes and laughter. My biggest fears were coming true...my church, the people who should love everyone, were making the cruelest of jokes and I knew deep down this was what I would face. As I found my way to a chair to wait for our next flight, I prayed and wrote this in my journal.

"We saw a transgender person today on our airplane. I knew when I saw him that the reality of going home and facing the new challenges we were now facing was going to hit me hard. This trip has been a great distraction for a few days. But the minute I saw him, I knew people would say something about it later. They confirmed my fears when we got off the plane and comments were made. The comments were in good fun, not meant for hurting anyone. How many times have I made comments without thinking about others' hidden secrets? Have I unknowingly hurt someone because of my insensitivity? Oh, forgive me Lord when the words of my mouth are not pleasing to You.

"Out of all of this, this was my biggest fear...people making fun of my child for decisions made. Oh, the hurt of a mother's heart. I am supposed to protect my child and now there is nothing I can do to shield the words and actions that will come. The mama bear in me wants to come out and scream at everyone, yet the silence brings comfort from the One I cling to, Who shines His love on my situation. I will smile, and forgive, and go on knowing it is just the beginning. The laughs and stares will always be there. Help me, Lord, to pray for my heart and theirs as we look at others. I pray for that boy right now and his mama who no doubt hurts as I do. Be their comfort, Lord, and may he see Jesus in someone today."

The hardest part wasn't their jokes. It was the deep sorrow I felt for what I had said and done through the years. The bigger problem here was that I had made fun of people too. I have laughed and told jokes and took part in behavior that isn't what someone who claims to know Jesus should do. The sorrow I felt was because of my own mistakes, not someone else's, and I knew this was just the beginning of the process God would use to transform my heart.

I had to look inward that day and repent of my own actions and forgive myself before I could ever offer forgiveness to anyone else. The work the Lord was doing in my heart was the first step in changing my heart to see others.

My favorite verse from this time was Psalm 19:14. "Let the words of my mouth and the meditation of my heart be acceptable in your sight, O LORD, my rock and my redeemer."

PRAISE SONGS AND HYMNS

That day I also began to realize that my church was way off on this issue and so many others, and my story's safety would not be found within the walls of a church.

How did church become a place where we could not share our struggles and hurts? When did it become a place where our shame had to be carried, not laid down? We talk about walking in freedom, but we smile, pretending it is well, while we are prisoners to our pain.

I pondered for a long time how we got here. Churches have changed. Worship has changed. One day, I was humming an old hymn to myself. As I sang the words silently, I realized that much of the gospel we once sang in old hymns had been replaced with praise songs…all full of God and His goodness and His love.

I love modern worship songs. I love singing to the Lord, but although we have gained so much freedom in our worship, we have lost singing the gospel that changes lives…the words that tell of laying down our shame and giving it to the Lord. We are singing half-truths. We are not telling the entire story…

brokenness and a Savior who can redeem it.

It's like when we study the Bible. We love to read the Gospels, throw in some Corinthians and Philippians, maybe even a psalm or two, and hit the highlights of the major Old Testament stories. We shy away from the hard things…like Revelation or 2 Kings and especially Leviticus. We convince ourselves we are a New Testament church, and we don't need to read the Old Testament law. Yet, if we do not understand the Old Testament law, we will never understand why we needed a Savior at all.

Leviticus is like the verses of an old hymn, and the grace of Jesus in Romans is like a praise chorus. The verses tell the story; they lay out the plan, the pain, the problem. Then the chorus comes in and solves what was wrong. There are two parts to the song, but God wrote them together as the complete song, and we need to sing the *whole* song.

As Christians, we get stuck on the praise chorus and don't want to sing about history. Or we sing verses 1, 2, and 4 because we don't like what verse 3 and 5 offer. We need to study the whole Bible because the One who wrote it is telling us a beautiful story…one complete, beautiful story. Old and new together, singing of redemption.

If pastors aren't talking about things like shame and brokenness, we'll never get to a point where we can share our stories. If we can't talk about the failures of our parenting journey, we will never successfully mentor the next generation of moms. Our churches must go back to being a hospital for the sick and broken, not a country club for the healthy.

Jesus came to take our shame. He took it and all our sins the day He was nailed to the cross and died for our sins. We do not have to hide our faces in embarrassment; instead, we need to speak up and share our struggles.

Hebrews 12:2 says, "looking to Jesus, the founder and perfecter of our faith, who for the joy that was set before him endured the cross, despising the shame, and is seated at the right hand of the throne of God."

Jesus took our shame upon Himself, so we could walk in freedom. We need to accept it and not look back.

Romans 8:1 tells us, "There is therefore now no condemnation for those who are in Christ Jesus."

None.

I love The Message version of this verse. "With the arrival of Jesus, the Messiah, that fateful dilemma is resolved. Those who enter into Christ's being-here-for-us no longer have to live under a continuous, low-lying black cloud. A new power is in operation. The Spirit of life in Christ, like a strong wind, has magnificently cleared the air, freeing you from a fated lifetime of brutal tyranny at the hands of sin and death" (vss. 1–2).

As a church, we must get back to sharing each other's pain and burdens. We need to learn to walk with one another, giving our shame to Jesus and carrying it no more. We must guard our mouths, not letting our words continue to shred the brothers and sisters we claim to love.

My friend Starla once told me about her church's Easter tradition. They have a cross set up and they give everyone flowers to pin on it, symbolizing what we can give to Jesus at the cross.

One year, as everyone waited in line for their turn to pin everything on that cross—their children, their hurts, their pain, their shame, their very futures—my friend noticed something. Someone's flower had fallen on the ground and everyone was stepping on it. This flower was once on the cross, but no one seemed concerned it was being trampled underfoot.

She approached the cross, bent down and picked up that flower and placed it back on the cross. She symbolically brought that person back to the cross of Jesus. She made the decision to refuse to let the flower continue to be trampled by members of the church till its beauty was unrecognizable. She knew that flower needed to be picked up and placed where it belonged, back on the cross of Jesus.

No matter what the rest of the church did, I knew I was being called to walk with other parents, picking up their shame, and helping them pin it to the cross.

I knew the Lord would need to work in my heart and life. I had to give Him control over everything I thought and spoke. He is asking you to do the same. The shame of our loss does not have to bury us; it can free us to trust in God to work out the entire story for His glory and our good.

PRAYER

Lord, thank You for the cross. Thank You that it is a place we can bring our shame and exchange it for Your peace. It is a place where we can lay things down, knowing the blood is enough to cover a multitude of sins.

Show me, Lord, how to bring my children to the cross each day, laying them before You. Help me to be a voice, showing others how we are trampling Your children under foot, children who have fallen away. Help us to pick them up before they become unrecognizable. Lord, You are the only One who can take our ashes and make them into something beautiful. Give me eyes to see others as You see them…not as lost causes, but lost children. In Jesus name.

7. PICK A CAMP

I NEVER PLANNED ON BEING a part of the church's LGBTQ discussion.

After finding myself in the middle of the contentious debate, I had so many tearful nights, trying to figure out where I fit in and what I believed. Would it be heaven or hell for my child? I would eventually have to pick which belief to run with. It is such a divided issue, and the pull to join one side or the other was immediate. I knew many in the church didn't see my child. They saw a political game and expected me to choose a side.

There are two distinct camps concerning the LGBTQ issue and the church. The first is the one I was the most connected to. It most matched my evangelical background. This camp that says the sin of being part of the LGBTQ alphabet is a choice, and that choice will send you to hell. It is the side that can clearly point out as many verses as they need to prove their stance. They use many clobber verses to justify their point of view. Verses like…

Leviticus 20:13, "If a man has sexual relations with a man as one does with a woman, both have done what is detestable. They are to be put to death; their blood will be on their own heads" (NIV).

Or Romans 1:27, "In the same way the men also abandoned natural relations with women and were inflamed with lust for one another. Men committed shameful acts with other men, and received in themselves the due penalty for their error" (NIV).

These verses and many others clearly state God's position. It leaves a parent of an LGBTQ prodigal feeling hopeless. Can hope, once lost, ever be found?

Then there is the camp that believes there's nothing wrong with being on the LGBTQ spectrum. It's the way God made them, they say. We should welcome every person, regardless of race, age, nationality, ability, sexual orientation, gender identity… and everyone should be able to serve in church leadership roles, without being told there is something wrong with them. This side believes the church should be a place where all are welcomed and accepted as they were created. The Scriptures, they say, are taken out of context, and translations have altered what God was saying.

The language used for these opposing views is affirming and non-affirming. I could literally pull up any church website and see the words they use and immediately know how they felt about the eternal security of my child. Both sides seem to think they get to a say who sits at God's table.

And I was expected to make a decision on where I landed on this issue. Would I pick door number one and stick to my strong evangelical roots and know my child had no chance of making it to heaven? Or would I choose door number two and embrace the emerging voice of the church that says they are who they are and because of faith, nobody is excluded? How could I decide?

If I went with the hell crowd, it meant possibly cutting ties with my child, and that was unfathomable. It felt like condemning my child to hell and not allowing for grace to enter the picture.

Alternatively, I was told that choosing the acceptance crowd would jeopardize my salvation. So now, not only did I have to worry about my child and his choices, but I also had to worry about whether God hated me for loving my child.

How can a parent possibly choose? It made zero sense how one day it was fine to love my child, and the day after the phone call I was expected to say something different.

Did I believe God loved him? Do I still believe it? Do I believe if I loved him, God would hate me? I had nowhere to turn for answers. How would I ever make any sense of this? Would my life ever be normal again?

One of the first things I knew I needed was community. I didn't know of any Christian groups for moms of LGBTQ kids, so instead, I found a secular group. This group fiercely believed in their kids, and they were very affirming.

I needed this. Not because I was going to agree with everything they posted, but I needed the emotional support of others wrangling with the newness of what I was feeling. I needed to be with people going through the same thing, who had the same questions, and most of all, had the same fears.

I quickly joined this online group and read many articles posted about kids on the LGBTQ spectrum. I learned a lot from this group in the early days. I needed to be reminded it was okay to love my child.

This group would be the source of so much information and questioning of my theology in the months to come. I am thankful they were there at the beginning of my journey to hold my hand as I navigated the new deep waters.

THE TWO EXTREMES

In the beginning, I spent a lot of time reading everything I could find. Some articles I found myself, and others seemed to find me. But there wasn't a day that went by that I didn't read an article about transgenderism.

The moms' group posted many articles as they worked to keep their members up to date on LGBTQ issues. I decided that when I read an article, it wouldn't just be for information. I would read it with eyes that were seeking the truth.

Each time I read a story, especially one that involved picking a side, I tried to see the gospel. I looked for where Christ showed up—not just His love, but His sacrifice on display.

If it was pro-affirming, I try to determine if it defined grace as a gift, because all of us radically need a Savior. If it was from a non-affirming perspective, I would look for evidence that they were keeping the arms of God's love open for everyone to accept. I looked for contradictions to His Word and filtered every article through God's love and what His Word said.

The saddest story I remember reading was of a trans-person who lived in California. After coming out to her conservative parents, they kicked her out and said they wanted nothing to do with her and her new lifestyle.

She was homeless for the next several years.

I now know, through a lot of research, that this story is so very common. Parents rarely know how to react, so they choose tough love. Unfortunately, that can mean life on the streets, drugs, prostitution, and crime…just to survive. The streets for this person were tough…so tough that in the end, she ended up taking her own life.

I'm sure this happens more often than we'd like to admit. Oh, how my mama's heart ached. I wondered what her last thoughts were. Did she remember her upbringing that clearly was in church? Did she cry out to God and ask Him to take this pain that was just too much to go on any longer? I was overcome with the loneliness of this child and how the church had turned their back on her. The church that is founded on the whosoever, told this child of the King her sinful choices were too big for Christ to overcome.

But that is not even the worst part of this story.

The worst part was after the body was found, they took it to the morgue where the next of kin was notified—the parents.

I can't imagine the pain of getting that call. So much time had gone by, and that sweet baby you once rocked to sleep was found deceased and alone on the streets. I can't imagine what went through their minds. But as the story unfolds, we learn the parents stuck to their word that day.

Their child's actions were so heinous they still wanted nothing to do with her. To them, serving God meant cutting out their child because of her choices…even in death.

The parents refused to pick up the body.

Refused.

Refused to offer the last act of love you can give a person, especially your child.

I read that and it broke me. Tears stream down my face even now as I remember reading that for the first time.

And this isn't a one-time thing.

This type of rejection happens all the time. According to a survey done by The Trever Project, 14 percent of LGBTQ youth say they had slept away from home because they were kicked out or abandoned, and 40 percent of those say it was because of their LGBTQ identity.

I don't even know where the gospel is in this story. Where is God's love that is bigger than our sinful selves? Where is the Savior who dined with sinners?

For as many articles as I was reading about non-affirming parents, I was also reading about affirming ones. This was also mind-blowing to me. It was more than "I love you and support whatever you want to become." It was full-on "get rid of all the old memories and forget your old life even happened." How do you erase the years of who your child was? I just couldn't understand.

One of the craziest things I read about was a family who so fully supported their child, that they threw a gender reveal party for them…so they could come out and announce to everyone what gender they had chosen. The party had balloons, cake, and photos. It was the total production. There was even a church ceremony reading the new name to the congregation and a re-baptism using the new name.

I was baffled. I understood supporting your child, but to go to this extreme. I couldn't get my mind around it. How could a family completely erase all the memories up to this point? How could vacations, birthdays, and baby book entries be completely forgotten?

It would be like erasing the best part of my life. As a mom, I often relive all my kids' childhood memories with great joy. I couldn't change them or forget them if I wanted to. They are a permanent part of me.

How could their church, which has an important role in making strong families and traditions based on the Word of God, participate in this confusion? I looked for where the gospel was in this approach. How could putting pride on display be something to celebrate in the church? That makes the grace they claim to not be transformative through the Spirit, but confirmative in the flesh.

These approaches to grace aren't radical, they're dangerous. When the church becomes a place where we are unwilling to call out contradictions to God's Word, we put ourselves in a place of loving people straight to hell.

WHAT SIDE TO TAKE

I didn't know where to turn. Those first few months, I sat with all this knowledge, wondering which side I was going to pick. It wasn't until one day while reading my Bible that the Lord spoke to me and reminded me Jesus didn't come so we would have to pick a side; Jesus came as the bridge between heaven and hell.

He already picked a side two thousand years ago. He died on the cross for my sins and your sins. His sacrifice wasn't so we could alter the gospel to make it say what we wanted. His sacrifice was so we could have eternal life. It was not the theology of either side that was wrong. It was the application of that theology that was mistaken.

If the non-affirming side genuinely believes that being on the LGBTQ spectrum is a sentence to hell, then shouldn't that spark a movement of love to actively pray for our children to come home?

Not once have I heard of a church holding a prayer service for prodigals. We call these precious children to repentance, but how can we get them at the feet of a loving Father if all we tell them is Jesus hates them? The basic command Jesus gave believers was to preach the gospel. That is an invitation for the lost. Jesus said He came for the sick, not the healthy (Luke 5:31). If their life choices are indeed a death sentence, then we can't stop at quoting verses about God's judgment of the sin. We must move to action. Our heart needs to break for the things that break God's heart.

And if the affirming-side people think there is nothing wrong with what is going on, then why do we need Jesus at all?

If Jesus came to overcome sin and death, and we refuse to acknowledge any sin in our lives, where is our need for a Savior? Accepting everyone and leaving them where they are isn't practicing the gospel, it's rejecting it. Any gospel that doesn't include laying yourself down and asking the Spirit to search your heart and make you a new person is false doctrine.

Maybe you have wrestled with these same views, not knowing what to believe. I've spent countless hours processing a theology I never imagined I would need. Which door I chose would change everything, and I could not see the heart of the gospel through either door.

That's when I felt the gentle nudge of the Spirit reminding me I did not have to go through either door the world had laid out before me. Instead, I could open door number three. This door allowed me to drown out the voices of others who tried to tell me what to think and offered me the opportunity to keep my eyes on Jesus. Friend, I'm here to say, you also don't have to pick a side. Let me say that again.

YOU DON'T HAVE TO PICK A SIDE.

Door number three says the love of Jesus is not for a side, it's for our salvation. It is available for everyone.

Revelation 3:20 says, "Behold, I stand at the door and knock. If anyone hears my voice and opens the door, I will come in to him and eat with him, and he with me."

The Bible is not horizontal, looking left and right. It is vertical to bring heaven to Earth. It is my salvation and yours. There is no limit to how many can accept this love and get into heaven. If I get into heaven, that doesn't mean someone else has to stay out. Love isn't divided because of a side; it's multiplied because of the cross.

Do not pick a side, just pick a Savior. You can't hate your child to heaven, but you can refuse to love your child straight to hell.

I am convinced that the gospel doesn't ask us to pick a side in loving our prodigals. In fact, the gospel is full of stories of what Jesus thought of them.

He loved them.

He came for them.

He died for them.

He invited them to sit at His feet.

Whatever we believe must be rooted in God's Word. The Bible

is not merely a book of stories we can look at and be happy. The Bible is a book of radical love that has the power to change us.

This Love came and died so we wouldn't have to stay in our sins. Love that came for *all* and is available to all. Love that chases down the lost, leaving the ninety-nine and looking for the one. Love that causes the angels in heaven to throw a party when that one comes back.

There is no one too far away from the Lord that they cannot come to a saving grace. We, as the church, cannot continue to align ourselves on a side of this issue based on man-made criteria. It's time we pray for the hearts of our children to come back to the Lord, and we move out of the way and let the Holy Spirit work.

THE BIG UMBRELLA

Whoever. I love this word. It is in so many of my favorite Bible verses.

"For God so loved the world, that he gave his only Son, that *whoever* believes in him should not perish but have eternal life" (John 3:16, emphasis mine).

"*Whoever* calls on the name of the LORD shall be saved" (Romans 10:13 NKJV, emphasis mine).

"*Whoever* dwells in the shelter of the Most High will rest in the shadow of the Almighty" (Psalm 91:1 NIV, emphasis mine).

Whoever is such a beautiful word. The definition according to *Merriam Webster Dictionary*, literally means "whatever person: no matter who."

No matter who. It's a radically inclusive word. A word that does not discriminate. A word that invites, justifies, calls. It is a word without shame and welcomes the weary. When I read it in the above verses, it gives a description of the gospel of Jesus. It does not pick a side.

The other day I read a new children's book called *The Big Umbrella*. The story is simple, yet it is a perfect image of our Father in heaven.

In *The Big Umbrella*, we see how there is always room for those who need shelter. The umbrella doesn't ask if you're tall. It doesn't ask if you're hairy. It asks nothing, but it only invites. It invites whoever. If you need shelter, come on in. There is always enough room. The umbrella is a safe place. A place to get out of the storms of this life. It is a place that saves us from the pouring rain and keeps us dry. Under it, drops are deflected. They hit the umbrella, and they roll off to the ground. Its protection is fierce.

When I read Psalm 91, I picture God's love as that umbrella. There is room for everyone under God's umbrella. The psalmist starts with this: "Whoever dwells in the shelter of the Most High will rest in the shadow of the Almighty" (Psalm 91:1 NIV).

Whoever. The invitation is there that we are all welcome to rest in God's love. He offers His love freely to all. It's a beautiful, poetic picture of how God promises His hand to be with us. The psalmist declares the mighty promises of God:

He is my refuge.

He is my fortress.

He will save us.

In Him, He will defeat our enemies.

In Him, we fear not.

He is our guard.

He is our protector.

He hears our cries and answers us.

He will deliver us.

In Him, we will be satisfied.

When I read these declarations, I can hear the Lord whispering to me, "These promises are for all My children."

I must confess I have been guilty of naming who is the whoever. Many, many times I have limited the whoever to the ones I feel it means. I have decided what that looks like. I have left out people, groups, you name it. If you did not fit within the image of whoever I thought, you didn't belong.

Somewhere along the line, I forgot how big of a whoever I was before coming to Christ. I lived with the idea that the umbrella was not big enough. Oh, but how wrong that is. The umbrella is big enough. Space under the umbrella is not divided; it multiplies. It is a space people run to in the storm. There is not a limited space that will run out if we let everyone in. No, the umbrella continues to spread out, so it can cover everyone. I love the last page of *The Big Umbrella*…

"There is always enough room."

Friends, may we remember that no side has the monopoly of God's love and forgiveness.

They are gifts. Gifts for all. Ephesians 2:8–9 says: "For by grace, you have been saved through faith. And this is not your own doing; it is the gift of God, not a result of works, so that no one may boast."

The *it* in this passage is inclusive. Grace, faith, and salvation are all gifts from Father God…gifts none of us deserve, yet they are freely given for everyone to accept. Our job is not to turn sinners out because of their lifestyle choices. Our job is to invite them in and lay them at the feet of Jesus.

There He can radically save them. The Holy Spirit alone will break off whatever needs broken off their lives. We cannot take on the job of deciding who gets to say yes. Our part is to welcome them in and allow for a work of the Spirit to change them.

Redemption is not a side; it's a Savior, and His name is Jesus.

PRAYER

Lord, I only want to speak Your words. Your words are life. They are true and they are sharper than any two-edged sword. May Your words cut through any preconceived idea I have of who You love and who can accept Your gift of salvation. Let my thoughts be Your thoughts and anything I do, be Your way, not mine.

Show me how to love people in grace, speaking the truth, never letting one letter of Your law fall away. Open the doors, Lord for the church to share the gospel with all Your creation. Let Your grace go into every community and let it change everyone it touches. In Jesus name.

8. WHAT IS A PRODIGAL?

FROM THE MERRIAM-WEBSTER DICTIONARY: Prodigal, noun, 1: one who spends or gives lavishly (wastefully) and foolishly, 2: one who has returned after an absence.

When we think of the word *prodigal*, our minds go to the Bible story in Luke 15 of the prodigal son. It's one of the most often told and retold stories from the Bible. The son squanders his inheritance by living on the wild side, comes to the end of himself, and comes back home. When he gets there, the father welcomes him home.

While it is a beautiful story of the forgiving Father God we serve, there is so much more God wants us to learn from this this chapter in Luke, and I believe He wants us to see ourselves as prodigals who have been found. God uses different parables in this chapter to show us that many are lost...just as lost as the son who wandered away on his own. He uses it to show us the extent He goes to bring every heart home, including mine and yours.

If you have a child or family member who has been a spiritual wanderer, you can relate to these parables. The church loves to tell the first three scenarios that deal with the outward sin of a lost child. It's so much easier to look at how lost someone else is and not think about how lost you might be.

But there is so much more to learn here.

Luke 15 has two different parables with examples of four different people who are lost and then found. One who willingly wandered away, one who was lost in the house, another one who wandered and couldn't find their way back, and one whose heart had wandered.

Jesus told parables, each outlining a different lost soul.

As the chapter begins, Jesus is sitting with sinners and Pharisees and the teachers of the law. It was not your normal dinner party. These groups did not mingle with snacks and Bible study. The religious among them couldn't grasp how Jesus was inviting all of the least of these to the table. Jesus knew He was making them uncomfortable, so he told them parables to reach through to their hearts of stone.

The first parable is of a lost sheep. Sheep wander. They go to find something to eat and before you know it, they have wandered off by themselves. Our kids are the same way. They didn't wake up one day and decide to wander. It's a slow process.

Perhaps they started hanging with the wrong crowd, or maybe they went to a party. Maybe they just didn't feel they were fitting in and started hanging out alone. Before they know it, they are with the wrong people, doing the wrong things, or alone and depressed. Their wandering happened without them even realizing they went astray.

Sometimes it is no fault of their own. Family struggles and health problems can lead them away from the Lord. Sometimes it's just easier to listen to the voice of Satan who tells them God doesn't love them anymore.

But God doesn't leave any sheep alone. He knows if the sheep isn't found, it will be attacked and killed. It must come back into the safety of the Shepherd's arms. He goes after the one that's lost and when it's found, He brings it home with joy. He calls others to rejoice with Him. We have found the lost sheep!

The Parable of the Lost Coin tells the story of a coin that was lost in the house because of carelessness. I like to think of a house as not just the place you live, but also the church.

Often, church is the place that turns people away from the Lord. It could be the judgmental glances or perhaps the country club feel that only certain people can belong. Whatever the reason, coins get lost in the house. Prodigals can sit in church each Sunday, and no one knows just how lost they are. They lost the coin in a house that was dark, and it wasn't until the light came in that they found it.

WE HAVE TO BE LIGHT

We need to care for others and seek the lost. Our heavenly Father never stops searching for these lost children, and so must we—even the ones sitting beside us each Sunday, sometimes in our own pew. We can't assume church attendance means someone wants a relationship with God. We have to engage on a deeper level to learn what struggles someone might be facing.

The final parable in Luke 15 is the Parable of the Lost Son. The first two stories center on the search for the lost. The last one talks about letting the spirit of the Lord stir in their hearts, bringing them back to the safety of the Father's arms.

The son in this parable is done with the rules of his house. He asks his father for his inheritance and takes off to live as he wishes. The son squanders the wealth in another land with wild living. Life was all good, living in sin, until it wasn't. Before he knew it, he was broke, alone, and out of options to survive.

That's the thing about living outside of God's will. Eventually, you tire of your own filth and know there must be more. The son had to get a job feeding the pigs. This would have been the worst of the worst jobs for a Jewish boy. It was not the father who went searching for the lost this time. The son remembered his loving father and his goodness and that brought the boy to repentance.

The boy wanted to come home but knew there was no way the father would forgive him and welcome him back. He practiced a speech to say to his father, begging to allowed to be a servant in his house again. His sins were many and he believed there was not way he could join his father's table again. He wanted to simply be as close to his dad as possible.

When the boy went home, the father ran out to meet him, forgiving him of all his wrongs and welcoming him back to the family. My favorite part is the son never spoke a word of the speech he prepared. His words didn't restore him to the father, the posture of his heart did.

If the story ended there, we could package up three tales of sinners who were lost and found, but then we would never really relate to the lost people, because we have never been in their place. We may have never wandered away or sat in a church we didn't fit in. Maybe we never willingly left our father's embrace and struck out on our own. If we stop at these three parables, it's hard to relate to the lesson.

But the story of the lost son did not end there. I love the NIV version of verse 25 which starts with *Meanwhile*. The whole parable is like a play, and we're now entering scene 2. Here we meet the prodigal's older brother. He is out working, just as he always has done—working hard, doing all that is asked. He probably volunteers to clean the church, teaches middle-school boys Sunday school, and builds sets and leads recreation for VBS. He is a prime example of a good church member. Compared to his brother, he is a saint!

The older brother gets off work and goes home to find a full-fledged party…music, a huge charcuterie board, and steaks on the grill from the grass-fed cow they'd been raising.

The brother is mad, hurt, and so angry at the father. He refuses to be a part of this. He states his case, reviewing for the father what an important, amazing part of this family he is. He never had strayed, nor had he even considered it. He spent his whole life sitting in a church. How could his lost brother be celebrated and restored to his former position?

The older brother was perfect on the outside. He did all the right things. He wasn't guilty of any outward sins, but his heart was far from the father. He was so wrapped up in what he thought the family should look like, he couldn't imagine letting his sinner brother back in. What would people think if I had to go to church with sinners?

The father assured the older brother all he had was his. There was room for everyone at his table. If we let a sinner in, it does not keep a saint out.

So many in the church are like that older brother. We don't want the sinners to show up. Not really. They don't deserve a second chance. When the lost sinner answers God's call and goes forward to weep at the altar...oh, the stares, the whispering. In many churches, altar calls are so rare that the first thing people think about someone praying at an altar is, "what did they do?" They are curious about the sins of others but are blind to their own.

How would the story have ended if the older brother ran out to meet his younger brother first? Would the younger son have turned around and never come back? Would he have been told he wasn't wanted anymore? Would the older brother tell him he smelled, and his clothes were awful, and he should turn around and stay away? It is what is happening in many churches. We gatekeep access to the only One who can change a heart, forgetting how awful our own sin is.

I love the definition of a prodigal that I gave at the beginning of this chapter—one who gives lavishly or wastefully. That is a grand description of our God. He pours out His love and forgiveness on all sinners, including me.

He is a prodigal's God. He will pour out every drop of love to bring a sinner to repentance. He lavishly gives His forgiveness and wastefully offers His love. The word *prodigal* usually describes our actions, but the best description applies it to God and His love. Oh, the beautiful waste of our loving Father!

As we pray for the lost souls of this world to come back to Jesus, we need to remember that we were once lost and have been found. We have to open our hearts to allow the least of these to come to our churches.

The days of playing happy country club church need to end. We need a hospital for the sick! We need to get over outward appearances and get back to inner transformation.

I was lost, but now I am found. Our kids are lost, but we long for them to be found. We long for the return celebration of a lost soul who has come home.

PRAYER

Thank You, Lord, for pouring out Your love on me. Thank You for chasing me down when I was far away and bringing me back to a relationship with You. Thank You for the beautiful waste of pouring out the blood of Jesus, so we all could be restored to the Father. Oh, Lord! Our world is broken, and we need You. We need Your love and forgiveness each moment. Don't let me forget You go after the lost and it is Your will that none would perish. Help me to see the lost as You see them… children not yet home. Here I am, Lord, send me where You need me to go. Open doors to preach the gospel to the lost world. In Jesus name.

9. WHY ARE KIDS WALKING AWAY?

SPRING YARD WORK. I cannot say I love it, but there is a satisfaction in picking up all of winter's garbage and preparing for the warm weather ahead.

It's one of the things that must be done, so I put on the headphones and spend the day picking up sticks, raking leaves, and planting flowers. There are always treasures to be found, seeing fresh growth coming from the dead plants of last fall, and I love seeing the promise of a perennial come back to life and the surprises the yard gives me.

One spring day when I was out picking up sticks, I discovered the most amazing thing—a hidden strawberry patch! We'd been in this house a few years and somehow, I missed the tiny treasure growing behind my shed. I've always wanted a strawberry patch, so finding this one brought me great joy! I ran into the house to share my find with my husband.

"It's not a strawberry plant. It's a weed."

What in the world?!

How was he so sure? After all, he hadn't seen these with his eyes like I had…they were the real thing. I just knew it. They looked exactly like strawberries. He had to be mistaken.

I had him go look again and sure enough, he pointed out

they weren't real. I was so disappointed and a little mad.

I pondered this fake strawberries revelation for several days. I still couldn't believe it. I even researched "fake strawberry plants" to find out what I could do with the ripe red fruits attached to this vine. Surely if they looked like strawberries, they would be as useful as strawberries.

My research, however, confirmed my fears. These berries were worthless and couldn't be used to make jam. They had no value. It disappointed me all over again. Why in the world is there a plant that looks like a plant I love, but has no value and is even considered a weed?

Mostly, I wanted to know how I could be so gullible that I fell for the plant's deception. I wanted strawberries so badly, I accepted the lie in front of me. My flesh overrode my brain, which knew full well a strawberry patch does not magically appear in your yard.

Determined to learn more about this trickery, I kept researching. I discovered that while the plants were similar, there were differences I would have noticed if I had studied the real thing more closely. Real strawberry blossoms are white, instead of yellow, and the leaves were different. Another big difference is that the mock strawberries are not as *hairy* as real ones. I could have avoided all this had I known all the characteristics of real strawberry plants. I could have spotted a fake a mile away.

This looks so much like our Christian walk and how the world sells deception, and our kids are buying it. Everyday the fake happiness and pleasures the world promises draw people away from God's table and into the world of sin and death. Just like me with the strawberries, they are easily fooled. The world promises happiness disguised as yummy strawberries, promising to fill every void in your life, never revealing that any lifestyle outside of the will of God leads to death. What the world is offering is not real, yet we see our kids running to it, settling for fruit that has no flavor or value.

So many of our children have fallen for it. How does this happen? How does the truth in God's Word not take root and produce eyes that can spot Satan and his lies? How does it happen that children raised in church turn to pleasures of the world and settle for the fake? How are they so easily deceived? What did I do wrong? What does the church do wrong in teaching our children what the actual truth is?

As I thought about all of this, I turned to Proverbs 7. It starts out with a gentle reminder, "Keep my commands and you will live" (verse 2 NIV).

This proverb is the reason we need to store up God's commands and teachings in our heart. It proves how easily the world is calling for our children, dangling fleshy desires in front of them. It warns about falling for fakes and the consequences. It speaks to our sin and how easily we can be lured into the trap of destruction. Solomon warns how evil is lurking, convincing the young man to go after his desires. She seduces him with promises of fleshly happiness and that their sin would be hidden and secret. This child was fooled, and the consequence was death. The chapter ends with "Her house is a highway to the grave, leading down to the chambers of death" (verse 27 NIV).

The reality of this proverb is revealed in the world today. How do we stay free from the entrapment of sin when the world tells us to live our truth?

The answer is simple. The Word. Storing the Word in our hearts will keep us on the right path. We'll know how fake the words of the world are when we know the truth of God's Word. The light of God's Word reveals the counterfeit.

Stay in the God's Word. Store up His commandments in

your heart. Know His Word and study it each day so you won't fall into deception.

HOW CAN WE RAISE CHILDREN
WHO WANT TO STAY?

When kids are young, it's easy to take them to church. However, studies show when they get older, many leave church attendance and the foundations of the faith we instilled in them.

Barna research in 2019 revealed nearly two-thirds of US eighteen- to twenty-nine-year-olds who grew up in church say they've withdrawn from church involvement as an adult after having been active as a child or teen.

Lifeway Research in 2019 also found that while 69 percent say they were attending at age seventeen, that fell to 58 percent at age eighteen and 40 percent at age nineteen. Once they reach their twenties, around one in three say they attend church regularly.

The research also noted the five most frequently chosen specific reasons for dropping out:
- moving to college and no longer attending (34 percent)
- church members seeming judgmental or hypocritical (32 percent)
- no longer feeling connected to people in their church (29 percent)
- disagreeing with the church's stance on political or social issues (25 percent)
- and work/school responsibilities (24 percent).

These statistics prove one thing: Satan is roaring around like a lion to devour our children and their heritage of faith. He whispers, "you have had a hard week, just sleep in this Sunday" or "Last time you went to church, everyone was looking at your hair color and outfit, judging you, you don't deserve that."

He convinces our kids they don't need those church people

in their lives, that they are out on their own now, making their own decisions and church doesn't need to be a priority.

Satan even uses employment as a reason to make attending church unimportant. He convinces us we need all the worldly things...new clothes, the latest phone tech, and so many other things. If you want to look cool, you must keep up with the trends!

So, with these staggering statistics, what can parents do to prevent their children from falling for the call of the world?

The answer isn't an easy one. I had to confront some lies I believed while raising my kids and in many ways and at many times I fell short. Not that I didn't try, I just put too much trust in a system instead of a Savior.

Sure, I taught my children about God. I would even say I taught them to love God. But it wasn't enough. I now know we have to change our approach.

We need to teach our kids to love God and love His holiness. They go together. I feel we fall short in this message to our kids. Maybe we've taught our children to love God and not seek His holiness, or we've taught just holiness without the love of God. Holy without love doesn't work and love without holy doesn't either. Our approach must be both if we want to see a lasting life transformation in them.

The world has always tried to pass off the fake as equal to something in the kingdom of God. In the story of the Exodus, we have Jannes and Jambres, the Egyptian court magicians who came against Moses. Three times Moses laid down a sign from heaven against Pharoh, they had an equally worldly sign, trying to prove their power and strength was equal to God's.

But on the fourth, they failed. No power of this world can duplicate the sovereignty of God. Not knowing what was real and what was fake was deadly for the Egyptians.

It is the same for our kids today. The world has all its appealing sparkly signs that appear to be real. The billboards the world flashes are these…

- Hell isn't real. A loving God wouldn't send people there.
- "Love is love," and God wants everyone to be happy.
- Blend in instead of being set apart.
- Everything falls under grace. You can live as you wish.

The world is lying, but our kids believe it.

The assault on this generation, if you haven't noticed, is on their identity. I have often said the kids of this generation want nothing more than a worldly label. They love them. I'm ADD, I'm LGBTQ, I'm OCD, I'm … etc. You get it. A label. Everyone has a label except the one that matters the most.

A child of the One True King.

We are in a spiritual tug of war between worldliness and godliness, and the lives of our children are at stake. It is no longer enough to just take our kids to church. In 2 Timothy 3, Paul talks about what the body of Christ will look like at the end of days. All the ungodliness will lead to death. We can no longer focus on the externals of religion and what that looks like, believing that is making an inward change.

The way we worship, the memorization of Scripture, the weekly rituals…none of it means anything if we don't teach true godliness, which stems from a personal relationship with God and His Son, and a life yielded to the Spirit in all things. We cannot continue to teach our children about God without knowing Him personally and knowing every letter of His Word.

We spend our time entertaining and over-training. The great theologian Charles Haddon Spurgeon once gave a sermon entitled "Feeding Sheep or Amusing Goats?" Reading the words of this would make you think it is from today, instead of the 1800s. I can only imagine what he would think of today's youth groups and children's programs. Even our Sunday morning worship services would make him turn over in his grave.

One of my favorite quotes from this sermon is, "An evil is in the professed camp of the Lord so gross in its imprudence, that the most shortsighted can hardly fail to notice it. During the past few years, it has developed at an abnormal rate evil for evil. It has worked like leaven until the whole lump ferments. The devil has seldom done a more clever thing than hinting to the church that part of their mission is to provide entertainment for the people, with a view to winning them."

What? Should it surprise us that our pizza parties, bounce houses, and smoke machines weren't enough to create real converts to Christ?

Spurgeon also states: "Lastly, the mission of amusement fails to affect the end desired. It works havoc among young converts. Let the careless and scoffers, who thank God because the church met them halfway, speak and testify. Let the heavy laden who found peace through the concert not keep silent! Let the drunkard to whom the dramatic entertainment has been God's link in the chain of the conversion, stand up! There is no one to answer. The mission of amusement produces no converts. The need of the hour for today's ministry is believing scholarship joined with earnest spirituality, the one springing from the other as fruit from the root. The need is biblical doctrine, so understood and felt, that it sets men on fire."

If we are going to win our kids to the Lord, we have to teach them about a Christ so personal that it sets them on fire! We can no longer tell our children they only need to add Christ to what they are doing, and they will have a complete life. We must tell them Christ is what makes them complete and without Him, they will have no life.

It's time we acknowledged that theme nights, VBS, and snow cone trucks aren't doing the trick in making disciples.

We have to get past putting on programs and get them into His presence. We must let the Spirit move again. Stop preaching a feel-good fun message to puff our kids up, and instead give them a life-changing message that will set them free.

I'm not against fun. I am the queen of fun! I love to plan parties and events. The answer isn't to cancel activities, it's to put them back in their proper place. It's time we got back to basics.

My prayer in all of this is as the apostle Paul said in Romans 10:1, "Brothers, my heart's desire and prayer to God for them is that they may be saved."

Our kids are leaving the faith, and we must figure out a plan to stop the exodus. We have to move from making converts to making disciples. I once read a quote that said, "Converts will run away, disciples are willing to die." The difference is standing on the sidelines or getting in the game.

Our kids should be in the game so deeply they won't quit at halftime when they have the chance. The finish line of eternity needs to be in them so deeply they won't stop till the race is over. They shouldn't just hear the Word, but live it!

We have work to do! We will not give up on our kids! We will not let the world sell them fake strawberries any longer. It's time to be about the Father's business…making disciples.

PRAYER

Lord, thank You that Your Word is true and that the more I read and study it, the more I will see everything in this world that is fake. Help me to have eyes to discern every fraud of the enemy meant to lure me away from walking closely with You. Help our children see the fake message of love and acceptance the world is feeding them and compare it with the Word of God, which is the truth. Give them eyes to see, Lord, and a heart to hear. Let them recall every sermon they have ever heard, every verse they ever memorized, and every worship song they ever sang. Bring all Your words alive in them, so they can spot the fake the world offers. Put your truth in their path so vividly that they can't deny it. Blind them to anything that will lead them away from You. In Jesus name.

10. PRAYER IS A VERB

I HAVE ALWAYS BEEN DRAWN to the Bible story of Moses and his birth. His mama's heart to save him is what touches me. In just eleven verses in Exodus chapter 2, we see how a mama trusted God with her precious child and how God answered.

This is how I like to picture this story in my head. Moses' mom, Jochebed, woke up that morning and knew it was time to float more than her child down the river, but her greatest fear—the same fear every mom faces—losing a child. I don't believe it was an ordinary weekday morning. I don't believe she got up, made breakfast, threw in a load of laundry, floated Moses down the river, went back home, and planned supper. I believe she focused the whole day on one thing—prayer.

I believe she got up that morning and the whisper of her heart said it was time to let Moses go and trust that God had him. She was obedient and prepared the basket, but placing Moses in the water was where her day really began.

She didn't go back home and make a casserole for her family. I believe she went back, locked herself in her prayer closet, and prayed her heart out. She prayed and cried with everything in her. I picture her flat out on her bedroom floor, crying out for God to save her child. I picture her repeating every promise back to God that had been spoken over this child. I can see her decreeing and declaring with authority over this situation. She knew the only way this baby was going to be saved was if God's own hand moved in this situation. She knew it and she believed He could do it. I can't imagine what that must have been like.

But I want to trust Him like that with my kids. I want to place them in the hands of God and let Him work. I want to pray with so much authority and confidence that the heavens are shaken. I want to use Jochebed as an example of a mama who believes and will not take no for an answer.

To get to where I needed to be, I had to look back at where I had been, fully examining my heart and my prayer life. I had to become a mom who prayed with authority. I had to dig in and figure out how to make the cries of my heart shift the atmosphere and bring change. I have often heard the phrase "never underestimate the power of a praying mama." I needed to become what that looked like.

The more I pondered my prayer life, the more I heard, "Is prayer a noun?" It was a weird thing to think because, well, I got a B- in English, and I hadn't thought about grammar in thirty years. I had to dig deep into figuring out what this phrase meant. I soon realized how prayer for me had just become a thing—something we say we are going to do. We think it offers comfort to others when we say we are praying for them.

It's words. Just words.

We have all been there, scrolling through social media and someone posts a problem they have, maybe an illness, or maybe a need. Reading through the comments, you will see a phrase on repeat…praying for you.

Now, I am not saying I know everyone's heart, but I know in my own life, I have been guilty of saying those words without even thinking about it, let alone praying like I said I would.

It has become a cliche…with absolutely no action.

How did we get to the point where prayer is simply a word, a phrase of comfort? When did it lose its action—it's power?

If we want to see what prayer truly looks like, we need to go to the book of Acts. The title of the book alone leaves no illusion that prayer is merely a word. It had a movement. A change. A response.

If I have learned anything over the last few years, it is how faith is easy when you don't need it. Faith isn't activated in the good times. It simply exists then. It's engaged in the trenches of living in a fallen world, fighting an enemy who has one purpose…to steal, kill, and destroy. Faith like that is not simply a noun…something that just is. Faith and prayer have an action behind them. It calls us to step out in belief.

Prayer is a verb.

Everything the church in the book of Acts did was based on prayer. Prayer is mentioned more than thirty times in those twenty-eight chapters.

We are told what they prayed for, when they prayed, and what happened when they prayed. We're even told how often they prayed. The details aren't there for us to skim over. God placed them there so we could grasp the importance of committing our lives to praying for our needs and expecting His answers.

But reading about prayer and changing the way I prayed was going to be difficult. I needed to learn and trust in this new season I was in.

PRACTICE

I was at a new farm store recently with some friends. The store had just opened, and it was situated outside of town on the old highway. As we stood outside looking at birdhouses, a normal peaceful day turned into an unexpected trauma.

A loud crash shattered the morning. We turned to the road in time to see a car bumper skidding down the pavement, followed by a motorcycle spinning out of control. A man tumbled after it, his body bouncing off the asphalt like a ragdoll before he finally coming to rest in a ditch. Seconds stretched into an eternity as we watched, helpless.

Shock barely describes the scene I witnessed. If you know me, you know I lose my junk in an emergency! House on fire…do not rely on me to get you out. An axe murderer chasing you, do not worry, you can escape because I will freeze and not be able to move, he will get me first. I have zero control in emergencies. My brain shuts off!

I stood frozen in shock, as my mind tried to process what I'd just seen. My legs refused to move for a few seconds, stuck between disbelief and action. Thankfully, the person with me didn't hesitate—they ran out to help and shouted, "Call 911." And there I was, staring at my phone, struggling to remember the numbers to 911!

As the man lay still, my mind raced to catch up. Was he alive? Badly hurt? Or worse? I held my breath, waiting for any sign of life. My legs were paralyzed, but my heart took over—I started praying! I claimed life over him, rebuking death with everything in me. Even if my brain couldn't process what had happened, my spirit knew exactly what to do. These were not wishy-washy prayers; I prayed with authority!

And then the man got up! This motorcycle rider, who had been struck on the highway, was now walking and talking. He was bleeding and dazed, but he was alive. I had just witnessed a genuine miracle!

Many people on the scene rushed to help that day. There was a nurse present, and an EMT was at the garden store as well. God always has people in place. The ambulance took the man to the hospital, and I prayed for his full recovery.

As the weekend went on, I couldn't get the scene out of my mind. I prayed many prayers, asking God to show me why He had me witness the accident and what I needed to learn.

He was teaching me about the process of becoming the parent of prodigals. One minute you're enjoying a nice day and the next, you're witnessing a crash, and your hopes and dreams are flying away. God was showing me I could be a powerful prayer warrior.

In my mind, I no longer saw a stranger on a motorcycle, but a family being torn apart by the unexpected…

- an announcement,
- a jail sentence,
- an alcohol problem,
- or simply changed values.

Maybe you've experienced a crash in your parenting journey. The sound of it is deafening. The impact on your dreams is brutal, and all you can do is stand back, helpless, as life unfolds in agonizing slow motion.

Watching your child roll down the highway of life feels like a slow-motion nightmare. You follow, eyes fixed on every point of impact, trying to gauge where the scars will be. The relentless force pushing them down this road seems neverending. With every injury, you mentally scramble for ways to help, yet deep down, you know there's nothing you can do. Nothing will stop this, and all you can do is wait, knowing they will eventually come to an abrupt stop.

When that moment comes, just as on that Saturday morning, you wonder if they survive the impact. As the seconds tick by after the crash, you hold your breath, waiting to see if they'll make it through.

My family is still in the roll. I don't know the outcome,

but the Lord taught me several things through that Saturday morning adventure.

First, crashes are unexpected and can happen at any moment. You didn't plan for it, and now it's changing everything. Even with all the lessons on how to avoid them, crashes still happen. In these moments, you have to trust God has your children and loves them even more than you do. Think of the story of Moses. The crash for Jochebed came when Pharaoh ordered all the male babies to be thrown into the Nile. She placed Moses in that basket, trusting his life with the One who loved him more than she did. The only way to save him was to let him tumble into the dangerous unknown. It was out of her hands and in God's.

Second, God has strategically placed people to help others on their journey. He already has them on the scene, ready to spring into action. Moses had the princess in the right place at the right time to draw him out of the water. God has people who will point our kids back to Him in their journey. He can and will use anyone He can to bring our kids back. His Word says He leaves the ninety-nine to go after the one who is lost. His eyes are always on them. He has provision in place.

Finally, we can call on Jesus. When nothing else makes sense, we can cry out to the Lord and declare life over our kids. Just as I did when the man was tumbling down the highway, we can rebuke death off them and declare they will live to tell about their redemption. Just as I believe Jochebed did as she placed Moses in the water. She prayed like life or death was in the balance, because it was, and we, too, need to pray like that.

A prodigal journey is tiresome, but, mama, God is still on the throne and still in control, and we will see our kids come home. Pray with the authority given to us, knowing Satan has already been defeated.

PRAYER

Lord, help me to trust You in each step of this journey. Help me to know You have someone at every step of the way, pointing my kids to You. When the crashes happen, help me to keep my eyes on You, walking and praying in the authority You have given me through Jesus. Help me to speak words of life over my situation and never stop believing You are bringing my children home. Wake me up, Lord, in my prayer life. Show me how powerful my prayers are and how they can shift the atmosphere. Help me never to doubt that my prayers make a difference. In Jesus name.

11. FORGIVING MYSELF

THE STORM WAS HERE. Blowing snow, icy wind, power outage. I did what any Midwest girl had to do. I went to the store for supplies.

I hate being that person who goes to buy bread, milk, and eggs, but snowstorms call for the making of french toast. Whatever I was making, I needed to go out in the elements, because I wouldn't be able to leave my house for days.

I ventured out on that winter white day and made it home with all the groceries. The snow was now coming down hard and I had one goal: make it into the house with all the bags at once. There was no way I was going back and forth to the frozen tundra of my driveway to retrieve more groceries. So, I grabbed all the bags and trudged toward the house.

What I didn't plan on was how I was going to magically open the door with my hands so full.

I struggled to free up my fingers from the bags I was juggling, desperately trying to turn the knob and get inside my warm house. No matter how hard I tried, I couldn't open the door. With my hands full, I faced a choice: put the bags down for a cozy escape inside or freeze outside while trying to manage the load and open the door. Of course, I knew what I needed to do.

If I'm honest, my walk with the Lord was just like that grocery bag struggle. The unexpected changes in my family dynamic shifted my life and my relationship with God. Just like that cold winter day, I had to empty my hands of all the burdens I carried and walk through the door to peace in Christ.

I was burdened by things God never intended for me to carry. I tried to navigate through God's peace and love, but the weight was overwhelming, and my hands were too full to move forward. To truly find freedom, I needed to let go of the lies I was holding.

Each step of my journey involved hard work, requiring me to die daily to my own desires and trust God with everything I loved. The final step to freedom was forgiving myself.

FORGIVENESS...IS IT POSSIBLE?

With God's help, I found ways to let go of jealousy, pain, embarrassment, church hurt, and so many other things, but the one thing that still had me frozen in place was forgiving myself.

I truly believed something I did, or didn't do, caused my family to look the way it does now. I was standing at the door in a blizzard while God offered me the warm embrace of His peace, but I had to empty my hands to step through. Forgiveness was the oversized box I clung to, shifting it from side to side, trying to make it fit, but it never did.

The final step to true freedom was letting it go. There was no other way to turn the knob and enter rest, trusting the outcome to God. Forgiving myself and releasing my perceived parental failures was what God called me to do.

I struggled with how I could truly forgive myself. I hadn't been a perfect parent—no one is. I knew that, yet I had somehow trapped myself in a prison of guilt, wondering if hating myself enough would somehow make God love my kids more.

I prayed and searched for a way out from under the weight I carried. I thought about God, the perfect parent, who also had children who strayed from His Word. He offered paradise to His first two children, and they chose to go their own way.

In the first two chapters of Genesis, God placed Adam and Eve in the ideal environment. They had it so good—living in a paradise with everything they needed! His plan was for all of us to live in perfect unity, free from sin.

Yet, chapter three reveals the truth: people have free will to make their own decisions, right or wrong. Sin entered the world with a simple doubt the serpent posed to Eve: "Are you sure?" That doubt shattered a perfect environment, leading to the fall of man and our need for a Savior. Adam and Eve chose outside the will of their Father, and because of that, God sent them out of the garden. What began as a perfect Father-child relationship turned into the story of a prodigal child. Even God, in all His glory, had children who strayed.

The serpent is still whispering that same doubt today to our kids and to me: "Are you sure God doesn't blame you?" This doubt has kept me stuck in hurt, paralyzed by guilt. I know in my soul the doubt I held created distance between me and the Lord. I couldn't fully enjoy the close fellowship I once had with Him because I listened to Satan's whispers: "It's all your fault."

God wanted to free me from this burden, so I dove deep into Genesis for answers. I realized something crucial: God did not blame Himself for Adam and Eve's sin. Nowhere do we see God saying, "This is all my fault. I should have been there that day, and I could have stopped them from eating the fruit. I should have done more."

God had two children and 100 percent of them became prodigals. Yet, God never blamed Himself. He put the responsibility where it belonged…on the children, and the punishment was to expel them from the safety of the garden out to where the struggles of life would be on their shoulders. God didn't take any guilt over His kids' actions…and we shouldn't either.

Parenting is hard. It requires so much faith and trust. I wasn't completely free from condemning myself yet. I was convinced I had sinned and failed so miserably as a parent that I deserved to be out of the garden, living in the wilderness alone. But God didn't put me out there. I did it myself, by carrying the weight of someone else's choices. I was bearing a burden God never intended for me, and my soul was heavy with the enemy's lies.

I had a decision to make. I stood at the door, ready to step back into a place of perfect peace. I could move into freedom and leave guilt behind, but that forgiveness required me to empty my hands and take a step forward. I needed help getting there, so I asked God to show me how.

FILLING UP

If I need to go somewhere in my car, I need gas. I won't get anywhere without it. The same is true for forgiving myself. The Lord gave me three steps to work on.

1. Go to the altar.
2. Ask your child for forgiveness.
3. Stand, then stand.

First, I had to go to the altar and surrender what I was holding onto. In every other area of my life, I accepted God's grace. He had forgiven me of all my sins.

The Bible clearly says all have sinned and fallen short (Romans 3:23), and I had accepted His gift. Yet, in this one area, I hadn't embraced His offer of freedom. So why was I letting the thought of not being a perfect parent block the truth of God's Word? I needed to get to a place where I could truly believe my sins were forgiven, even in this.

This is where Satan tries to keep us down. If he can convince us to cling to our unforgiveness, he can keep us out of the garden of peace. I had stayed outside the garden because I believed my guilt would somehow help bring my child back. How wrong I was.

I needed to ask God for forgiveness for holding onto the idea that it was all my fault. I had to forgive myself and let my heart be set free from the guilt I carried, so He could fill it with His peace.

Going to the altar was a step forward. I knelt and told God I forgave myself. I prayed, "Lord, I know You can take the crumbs of my parenting and turn them into something beautiful. I trust every piece can be used as part of Your plan. I'm sorry for the things I should have said or done but didn't. I'm sorry for the times I didn't make the best decisions. Yet, I believe You will use all things for our good and Your glory. You hand-picked me to be the mom to my babies, knowing exactly what I would and wouldn't do. You chose me to be their mom, and I rest in knowing I did the best I could. When I feel short, I rest in Your grace to fill the gaps. Forgive me, Lord, for not trusting You knew what You were doing when You gave these children to me."

The next step was to ask my child for forgiveness. I needed to acknowledge to my child the things I wished I would have done differently. Parents are human. We make mistakes.

If you know there are things you need to apologize for, do it. Be honest with your child. If there are specific situations where you fell short, acknowledge them. If you have a relationship with your child, go to them and be upfront about your mistakes. Don't hesitate. If contact isn't possible, write a letter—mail it or save it for a future opportunity. Release the guilt and allow yourself to find peace.

The last step in moving forward was to stand…then stand. Satan knows if he can keep our hands (and hearts) full of anger, jealousy, hurt, and unforgiveness toward ourselves, we won't be able to move forward to believing in miracles.

Ephesians 6:11 says to withstand every attack of the devil we need to put on the whole armor of God. The *whole* armor. If we are carrying the weight of unforgiveness, our hands are too full to put on the armor…and without our armor. we are unprotected.

Satan knows if you are wearing your godly armor you will be able to fight him off. We wrestle not against flesh and blood but against principalities, against powers, against darkness (Eph. 6:12).

If we're going to fight this battle, we must empty our hands of emotions and fill them with weapons of war.

My favorite verses in Ephesians 6 are verses 13–14a. "Therefore take up the whole armor of God, that you may be able to withstand in the evil day, and having done all, to stand firm. Stand therefore."

The apostle Paul mentions *standing* twice. It starts with putting on the armor. The armor is not jealousy, hurt, unforgiveness, and pain. You can't fight the battle of losing your family with walls you put up and lines in the sand you have drawn.

Spiritual battle requires armor and weapons of war from the spiritual realm to protect yourself. If you're not protected, you are no use to God in His war. You're a weak target. The enemy will take you out.

I almost let the enemy win by not forgiving myself. He had me so weighed down I couldn't imagine a victory. Paul tells the Ephesians: "Having fastened on the belt of truth, and having put on the breastplate of righteousness, and, as shoes for your feet, having put on the readiness given by the gospel of peace. In all circumstances take up the shield of faith, with which you can extinguish all the flaming darts of the evil one; and take the helmet of salvation, and the sword of the Spirit, which is the word of God, praying at all times in the Spirit, with all prayer and supplication" (vss. 14–18).

We need these things, and I love how Paul says to put all this on to stand in the faith ready for battle…then, after doing your part by making yourself braced and ready…let go and stand firm that God has it.

STAND. THEN STAND.

The first stand requires action; the second requires faith. I know how tough this is. I struggled for a long time to release unforgiveness toward myself. But once I laid it down and fell into the forgiving arms of Jesus, the weight was gone. I was finally free from Satan's whisper that my situation was all my fault. Releasing everything to the One who holds our children was the hardest part, but it was what I needed for the battle facing me.

If unforgiveness toward yourself is keeping you from moving forward in peace, I pray you pour some faith-filled fuel on your spiritual journey. The Lord is faithful to hear us and answer us. Our parenting journey isn't over—it's just beginning.

Satan no longer holds me. He is a defeated foe.

PRAYER

Lord, help me to forgive myself for any parenting errors I've made. Show me what I need to ask forgiveness for from You, and give me the courage to have an honest conversation with my child, asking their forgiveness as well. Remind me that hating myself doesn't lead my child to love You more; it only keeps me from a closer walk with You. Help me release the shame I've carried. Help me open my hands and surrender the pain I've held into Your loving arms. In Jesus' name.

12. SPEAK UP

SHARING HAS ALWAYS BEEN HARD FOR ME.

I'm not one to open up about my thoughts, struggles, or personal life. When my world changed, I heard Satan whispering, "Never tell your secret."

I believed his lies about needing to carry this burden alone. He told me if Christians knew, they would reject me, so I kept the secret. While my close friends knew, I kept my family dynamics hidden from new acquaintances.

I felt ashamed, but it wasn't about someone else's actions. It was about my own perceived failures as a parent. Why was it so hard to admit I didn't raise perfect Christian kids? The shame was always about my parenting mistakes.

Recently, I joined a new Bible study and grew close to the ladies there. I loved walking with them through the challenges in our lives, yet I never shared my personal struggles. It was too difficult, too uncomfortable, too "not churchy." The issue wasn't their potential judgment but my own shame and the lie that I had to go through all of this alone.

One night our conversation turned to LGBTQ issues. I sat in silence, feeling the pain of the discussion, wanting to shout, "YOU'RE TALKING ABOUT MY FAMILY! YOU HAVE NO IDEA HOW HURTFUL THIS IS!" As the conversation unfolded, I heard the true feelings of these women I had come to care for. Some mentioned sending their children to Christian schools to avoid "those kids." I was in tears, realizing I couldn't keep my secrets any longer. I needed to speak out, not to gain allies, but to align with God's truth.

It was more than an emotional reaction; it was a pivotal moment. I discovered my voice—one God had given me to speak truth in love, not to hide in shame but to express grace. I realized I needed to hold my head high, speak God's Word with authority, and proclaim His love for all His children. Something inside me awakened, and I knew it was time to speak up.

Leaving that Bible study, I resolved to shed the shame and be open with other Christians about my journey. It was time to stop hiding and overcome Satan's lies that I was alone and failing as a Christian parent. I went home that evening feeling broken, but also determined to trust that God, who had brought me this far, would use my voice to help others.

And I kept thinking about the story of Esther.

Esther was a young girl who had to find her voice and believe God was with her, in order to save her people. The salvation of the entire country rested on her shoulders. In the process of coming to terms with her calling, her cousin Mordecai challenged her with these words: "For if you keep silent at this time, relief and deliverance will rise for the Jews from another place, but you and your father's house will perish. And who knows whether you have not come to the kingdom for such a time as this?" (Esther 4:14).

Esther had a choice, and I did too. Was I going to let this bury me and never share again, or would I allow God to raise me up to have a powerful voice on this not so popular subject? I broke down this verse to find my answer.

"For if you keep silent." God was giving me a choice. Could I

be the one to offer hope and walk through the dark places with other moms, moms like me, who feared what others thought about their parenting? Was He calling me to a place not to handle what I was going through alone, but to learn to hand it over and let Him make beauty from my ashes?

"Relief and deliverance will rise from the Jews from another place, but you and your father's house will perish." It was time for someone to step forward and speak. I had never met another Christian family who talked about having prodigal children. I needed someone to be that voice, and God was telling me it would be me.

Twenty years earlier, God gave me a dream that I would one day stand on a stage and speak. Many nights, I awakened after the dream and wonder what in the world I would speak about. I was now finding out.

Those dreams were becoming reality. I never imagined sharing my pain with anyone, but I knew if I didn't, God would find someone else, leaving me to live in fear, defeated by the enemy in my thoughts. The choice was clear: let God work through me or miss out on what He intended. Doors began to open, and it was up to me to step through and be part of His plan.

"And who knows whether you have not come to the kingdom for such a time as this?" Maybe this wasn't a shiny ministry or a happy subject, but if I wasn't true to the story God had given me, He couldn't use me to do anything else. He was assigning me to lead a movement of praying moms believing for the return of their children.

God also took me to Jeremiah 12:1–4.

JEREMIAH'S COMPLAINT

"Righteous are you, O LORD, when I complain to you; yet I would plead my case before you. Why does the way of the wicked prosper? Why do all who are treacherous thrive? You plant them, and they take root; they grow and produce fruit; you are near in their mouth and far from their heart. But you, O Lᴏʀᴅ, know me; you see me and test my heart toward you. Pull them out like sheep for the slaughter, and set them apart for the day of slaughter. How long will the land mourn and the grass of every field wither? For the evil of those who dwell in it the beasts and the birds are swept away, because they said, 'He will not see our latter end.'"

Jeremiah was complaining to God about the wicked in the land and was crying out to God to do something. When Jeremiah got done, God answered.

"If you have raced with men on foot, and they have wearied you, how will you compete with horses? And if in a safe land you are so trusting, what will you do in the thicket of the Jordan?" (vs 5).

God was saying, "Jeremiah, if you can't endure this trial, you will never survive what is coming."

He told me the same thing. If this caused me to stumble so much I was silent with eight people at a dinner table, then I would never be able to stand on a stage and speak about the goodness of God.

Instead, He called me to hold my head high and walk through every door He was about to open.

Revelation 12:11 says, "And they have conquered him by the blood of the Lamb and by the word of their testimony, for they loved not their lives even unto death."

Telling my story mattered. It mattered to God and was the key to overcoming my pain.

STORIES MATTER

Stories matter to God. People matter. The Bible is full of true stories of real people with colossal problems. There are long stories told in chapters and then there are shorter stories. My favorite minor story is one-line, Judges 3:31, "After him was Shamgar the son of Anath, who killed 600 of the Philistines with an ox goad, and he also saved Israel."

One line. This is all Shamgar got. Other judges like Deborah, Sampson, and Gideon got entire chapters. Shamgar…he got one line. Why in the world is this here? What can we learn from it? I had to find out.

As I read this line over and over, God told me this wasn't just about the life of Shamgar, it was about my life. Eventually, Shamgar taught me four things:

First, he offered God his willingness. Shamgar did what he needed to do and was a vessel God could use for His purposes. Was I willing to do the same? Could I say, "here I am, Lord, send me" and not be mad if it wasn't to the shinier people?

Secondly, Shamgar used what God gave him. He had an ox goad, a common farming tool, that he knew how to handle. He did not use excuses; he used the tools God gave him. God gave me a voice to speak and a hand to write. It was time to offer those to God to see what He was going to do.

Then, Shamgar stayed true to who he was. He didn't argue with the Lord about not attending warrior school or finishing his leadership courses. He simply said, "I'm ready." I couldn't argue about what God called me to do. I simply needed to say, "I'm ready." God called me to be me…not anyone else. He knew the gifts He had given me and my heart to see the lost saved. I had all I needed to do whatever work God wanted me to do.

Lastly, Shamgar's yes had a kingdom impact. He saved Israel. My yes to God to fight for the lost would have kingdom impact. A surrendered life has kingdom impact for generations.

It was time to let God use my story. I had to quit asking *how* to get out of this and change it to *what* can I get out of this. My child was transgender, but I was the one who changed. I became who God made me to be. A warrior. A warrior who could lead a group of praying moms and change generations. And a warrior who believed God was bigger than anything we face.

I wanted to look at that verse in Judges and put my name in it. If that was written today, I wanted it to say, "Then came Debra, daughter of Thelma. She prayed with all that was in her and believed the prodigals would come home. She used her voice to offer hope, lead a movement, and help win our children back. She helped save a generation of spiritual wanderers by believing God could and would save them."

God got my voice ready to use. My story would win souls and offer hope. It was time to come out of hiding and walk in freedom. You, mama…your story matters. He needs us to speak up in this hour, declaring His truth. It's time to surrender our voice and see what God will do.

PRAYER

Lord, thank You for the voice You have given me. Help me to walk through each door You open, speaking about the words You would have me speak. Help me not to hold my head in shame, but to bring my story to the light, where the healing can happen. Help me as I share my struggles with the body of Christ and speak boldly about the secrets of my heart. Remind me, Lord, that Your church is a hospital for the sick and not a country club for the chosen. Let my story be the light someone else needs to see. In Jesus' name.

13. NOT ON MY WATCH

FROM THE BEGINNING OF MY JOURNEY, I realized this was going to be a fight. One that I refuse to lose. The road is hard for parents of prodigals. Many Sundays, I have sat in church, looking around wondering if anyone else has prodigals. Are they as broken as I am? Do they know they're not alone?

I want to stand up and shout, "SATAN IS NOT GETTING OUR KIDS!" The cry of my heart is strong, but my faith is weak. I wonder will the truth of God's Word ever penetrate the dark places of a lost one's heart?

The strongest part of the enemy's lie is that we are nothing. He whispers we are weak and alone. He convinces us we don't have it in us to fight this fight. He tells us our kids walked away from the Lord because of something we did—or didn't do—and there is nothing we can do about it now.

But I am here to tell you, there is something we can do about it. The fight God put in you is enough. You are not alone, and you can fight this battle.

I love the story of Gideon. The Old Testament judge started out as a weak doubter, but God turned him into a mighty warrior who saved the entire nation of Israel. He thought he was weak and that God could not possibly use him.

I love that God includes stories of weak people who have doubts about His Word…people just like me!

The story of Gideon unfolds like this…Israel had done evil in the sight of the Lord. So, for seven years, He gave them into the hands of the enemy. But it was time for the Lord to deliver them, and He chose the least likely person to do it.

GIDEON

The struggle was real for Gideon. Satan had whispered "you're not enough" so many times that even when God called out to him, he couldn't believe it. And God, being the loving Father He is, met Gideon in his doubts. He patiently gave him the proof he needed, not out of obligation, but out of love.

I have to believe God did it because He knew the coming victory would be so strong and the harvest so amazing there could be no room for doubt in Gideon's mind about who he was in God's eyes. God met Gideon in his pit of doubt and lifted him to the mountain of truth.

He'll do the same for us.

God knows every parenting failure, every tear shed in the dark, and every weight carried from our children's choices. He knows the cries of our hearts and the questions that haunt us. He knows our weaknesses, but He doesn't leave us there to drown. His love rains down, washing away the lies of the enemy.

He won't leave us in our doubts, scared of the future, because He knows the battle we are in is too important. He's waiting for us to get into the fight and stand in victory by praying for a generation to come home.

As a parent, I have these same doubts about my calling. I've failed. I've cried myself to sleep more nights than I can count. Like Gideon, I've bought into the enemy's lies—that I have no worth, that this mess is somehow my fault, that I've been outside of God's will all these years and now I'm getting what I deserve. Maybe you feel the same way, wondering how you can offer hope to others when you're struggling to find enough faith just to get out of bed.

But Gideon's story doesn't end there. God shows up and speaks truth over him. He comes to remind Gideon who he is, and He comes to remind me—and you—who we are.

I am not the sum of my parenting mistakes. I am not defined by my circumstances. I am not powerless in the face of my children's choices.

Even when Gideon was filled with fear and insecurity, God called him a mighty warrior. That's what He calls you too. You are not a failed parent. You are not a weak Christian.

YOU ARE A MIGHTY WARRIOR.

Let me say that again…YOU ARE A MIGHTY WARRIOR!

The Lord needed Gideon to understand who he truly was and what was within him. Gideon didn't realize he had the strength to break the generational curses in his own family. He didn't understand that, in accepting his calling, God would use him to destroy the idols that had dominated his family for years. He didn't know his faith would impact his children, grandchildren, and even his great-grandchildren. He didn't foresee leading a small army of three hundred to defeat a massive Midianite force. Gideon only saw his weakness, not the calling God had placed in him or the incredible harvest that lay ahead.

And that's exactly how Satan plays the game today. He wants to keep us trapped in our pain, convinced there's no way out. He doesn't want us to realize we have a calling—that if we grasp what God has put in us, we can call a generation back home. We might be few, but we are a mighty army of parents who refuse to let this generation be lost. If we truly understand who we are in Christ, we can push back the gates of hell. We have the power to pray our prodigals home. We need to grab hold of what Gideon's story teaches us.We are who God says we are, and we can do what God says we can do. The Spirit in us is greater than the enemy whispering to us. "He who is in you is greater than he who is in the world" (1 John 4:4).

If we can walk in this calling, nothing is impossible! Wake up, mighty warrior, the battle is on.

FAITH TO MOVE MOUNTAINS

We can believe these truths are for us, and we too, can see the victory. We can pray and believe with power and remind Satan he is *not getting our kids*.

If we are going to win this battle, we're going to need faith. Not any kind of faith, but bold, pushing-through-the-crowd, I'll-look-like-a-fool-and-do-whatever-it-takes type of faith. We find one of the best examples of this in the story of the paralyzed man in Luke 5:17–26.

"On one of those days, as he was teaching…the power of the Lord was with him to heal. And behold, some men were bringing on a bed a man who was paralyzed, and they were seeking to bring him in and lay him before Jesus, but finding no way to bring him in, because of the crowd, they went up on the roof and let him down with his bed through the tiles into the midst before Jesus. And when he saw their faith, he said, 'Man, your sins are forgiven you.' …he said to the man who was paralyzed—'I say to you, rise, pick up your bed and go home.' And immediately he rose before them and picked up what he had been lying on and went home, glorifying God. And amazement seized them all, and they glorified God and were filled with awe, saying, 'We have seen extraordinary things today.'"

I picture the scene like this: The friends arrive, carrying the guy on his mat. Maybe he didn't want to go. Maybe he was telling them to stop and take him home the whole time. They didn't know what would happen, but they knew the only way to see a change was to get their friend in front of Jesus. Laying him at His feet was the only fix to his situation.

But there were so many obstacles. So many had gathered to hear Jesus that day. There was no chance they were getting in. So many others had gotten there first. Maybe they waited all night to get a front-row seat. Maybe they were friends with the owner of the house, and that entitled them to come in first. Maybe they were big financial supporters, and that gave them a front-row seat.

It's like when you go to a conference and they reserve the first few rows for VIPs because somehow, important people need to sit in front. What we do know is that many Pharisees and scribes were there listening to Jesus that day, and such a large crowd had gathered outside the four friends had no way of getting in, no matter how hard they tried.

Yet, these friends didn't take no for an answer. They were determined nothing would stop them. If they couldn't get in through the door, they would go through the roof. Can you imagine the looks on the faces of the people in the house? Here they are, sitting in front of Jesus, and suddenly, a guy drops through the roof, grabbing Jesus's attention.

They had to be absolutely annoyed!

We don't know much about the paralytic man. Was he paralyzed in an accident? Did he make poor decisions? Did he get himself into this mess and deserve to be in this position?

So many questions and not a lot of answers, but we know this…One minute at the feet of Jesus and his entire world changed. Jesus didn't look at this man's outward appearance and the scars all the world could see. He looked at the man's heart and the faith of his friends.

The people in the house weren't concerned with this man's healing. They weren't concerned with faith issues, but law issues. Healing took a back seat to their rules.

It looks so much like the state of the church today. Jesus came for the sick, not the healthy, but we expect the lame to come in healed before they ever meet Jesus. We've kept people out of our churches because they don't look, talk, or dress like us. We have such tight circles and rules based on what we see, that those prodigals needing healing, especially the LGBTQ, will never be allowed access to the Great Physician.

One night, I went to a concert with my daughter at a large Christian university. When the concert was over, we joined thousands of other people as we headed back to our car parked in a large lot. If you've ever been to a large event, you know the dreaded parking lot scene and you know you're going to be there a while. You might as well accept your fate.

This night, though, something happened. As we sat and waited for our turn to pull out, we heard shouting. Now, remember we'd just spent two hours worshipping in the presence of Jesus. It was a beautiful night where souls were touched. But now, minutes later, praise had shifted to shouting.

There were two cars, and they both wanted out. One was an average car with younger drivers. The other was a very nice car with a well-dressed man, probably in his forties. By the looks of his car, we assumed he had a pretty good life. The younger group had pulled out in front of this nice car, and the driver was not happy. During the shouting match, these words were uttered, "I've paid good money to this institution."

And there it was. It made his status known. He assumed since he was a supporter of this Christian school, he should be at the front of the line. Maybe he was a graduate, and perhaps his kids were graduates as well. Maybe he had his name on a brick or on a plaque, letting the world know how big of a financial supporter he was. All we know is he thought his status gave him first rights of getting out of the parking lot that evening. The gifts he gave the school deserved the favor he expected. He shouldn't have to wait in line with normal people.

His heart was so much like the heart of the Pharisees in the house with Jesus that day. He heard the words from the songs that night. Maybe he sang along. Maybe he raised his hands. Yet the words never got through to his heart. He was stuck on being the greatest and not the least. In that moment, he missed the whole point of the gospel, just like the Pharisees in the house missed the gospel. The presence of Jesus in front of them did not change them, it challenged them.

Yet the beauty of the story of the paralyzed man is the faith of the four friends. Nothing stopped them in getting their friend at the healing feet of Jesus. I must wonder, though, about the people who were already in the house. Why didn't they clear the way and make room for this person who obviously needed Jesus? Did they think their money, or their status, or their gifts somehow entitled them to get to Jesus first?

And I am reminded of my heart. How many times have I kept someone from seeing Jesus?

That day, Jesus didn't ask who got there first. He didn't ask to see the giving records of the attendees. He didn't ask who memorized the most verses. He only saw faith, and faith was rewarded.

When I think about our prodigals and what their lives look like, I wonder: What will it take to get them at the feet of Jesus?

We will have to fight through a religious crowd that will try to keep us out and say our prodigals do not belong. The fight will require a strong faith. We'll have to stand strong, as one voice, and climb some roofs when the way is blocked. We will have to believe God has called us *mighty warriors*, just as He did Gideon. We'll need to remember who God says we are and that we can do what God says we can do. We'll have to fight our way in, but the result is to lay our children down in front of the Healer of their souls.

The battle for our kids is on, and Satan *will not get our kids*. We'll get them before the Lord, laying them all at His feet. We will fight this battle in prayer, and we shall not lose.

PRAYER

Lord, help me to become the warrior You made me to be. Help me to rise and fight for a generation that is lost. Show me every gift You have given me and how to use them for Your kingdom. Help me get a generation of children in front of You and not stop until they are. Move any obstacles that would keep me from bringing my child to You. Send me mat carriers who will fight for me, moving the crowd so my child can come. Put a mighty community around me, holding me up when I am too tired to go on and cheering me on in the fight. In Jesus' name.

14. IDENTIFY THE ENEMY

I HAVE A CONFESSION. I flunked my driver's test.

I've been driving for thirty-five years and I don't know how it happened. What I do know, is that my failure has provided my family with endless teasing opportunities.

How does someone who has been driving almost forty years not pass? Here's my theory.

We're movers. Our family has lived in six different states and moved nine times during the last thirty years. There's a lot of excitement, or shall I say anxiety, that comes from moving so often.

There are the normal things that come with moving…

- finding a grocery store,
- meeting people,
- finding a church,
- getting your mail to arrive in a timely manner,
- don't even get me started on finding new friends.

And then, there is the one thing that gets me…EVERY. SINGLE. TIME.

It's the black cloud that looms over my head that says, "Time to get a new driver's license."

I've learned over the years that every state has its own rules. Some states let you use the driver's handbook, so it is more of an open-book kind of test. I love those states! Praise ye the Lord!

Some states believe the license you had from the last state you lived in is enough proof you can drive, and they just take your old license and throw a new one at you. Again, all glory to Jesus the King! However, there are those states that welcome you with…"Welcome to our state. Now prove you can drive."

That is the welcome I got in our last move.

I'd heard rumors from my new neighbors that many people do not pass the first time. "Ha!" was my response to that. How hard can it be? I have decades of driving experience, just give me the test. I do not need to study.

The joke was on me.

On the day of the test, I sat in the room waiting. I saw a few other people who walked to the counter in what I now know is the walk of shame, confessing to the attendant the computer had told them they didn't pass.

I started getting nervous. I had done nothing to prepare. Maybe I should have reviewed a few things before coming in. They called my name and I gave myself a pep talk. I had this.

What I really had was one hundred questions, many of which I didn't know. Some of them were easy peasy. Others were trickier and I struggled to remember the answers. I had been in just about every driving scenario in real life, and I knew how I handled it, but was it the right way? I'd soon find out.

Eventually, the computer kicked me off and said, "Take the walk of shame to the counter and try again later. You're a loser. Have a good day."

That may not be exactly what it said, but close. I walked out of that place, knowing I didn't know enough to pass the test. It sent me into a study session I hadn't experienced since college, so I would be better prepared for next time.

I went home and pondered for days, trying to figure out how I missed so many questions. I'm an excellent driver. I know the law. I don't speed. I don't drive recklessly. How did I go from knowing the law to knowing enough to drive yet not being able to answer questions about it?

Years of driving without accidents or tickets made me think I knew exactly what the law said. I thought my knowledge was enough and let my feelings dictate what I thought the law was.

The more I pondered this, the more I realized this was true in other areas of my life…expecially with God and His Word. I allowed years of life experience, bad theology, and lack of studying the Word for myself to lead me to believe the happy things about God's Word and not focus on the scarier things like demons after our children. My lack of real knowledge about the enemy of my soul lulled me into being lax in my prayers in this area.

Yeah, I knew there was an enemy out there. I could even quote Bible verses reminding me of him…

"Be sober-minded; be watchful. Your adversary the devil prowls around like a roaring lion, seeking someone to devour" (1 Peter 5:8).

I believed spiritual warfare exists, but what I didn't believe was that it would happen to me. I didn't not know enough about what God says about the enemy seeking to destroy our families. I didn't arm myself with knowledge of God's Word to fight a battle and I didn't even know that battle was coming. The test came to my doorstep, and I flunked because I wasn't prepared.

I did everything right. I went to church, read my Bible daily, prayed, and led a solid Christian life. Why would I have to worry about Satan bothering me or my family? I am covered by the blood of Jesus. Nothing would touch me.

But the phone call made me realize I had not studied enough for my parental driving test, and I had failed. The enemy is real and after our families. What I failed to realize was that I had authority over him, and I could take authority over my family. I had to study harder, deeper, and come to a better understanding of who Satan was, what he wanted, and what his plans were. I also needed to study what God says about him and what I could do to defeat him.

I went to Genesis. Satan makes an appearance within days of creation being complete. He started whispering lies to Eve.

Genesis 3:1, "Now the serpent was more crafty than any other beast of the field that the LORD God had made. 'Did God actually say, "You shall not eat of any tree in the garden"?'"

There you have it. Satan deceived God's creation through one simple tactic: doubt. He caused Eve to doubt with the question, "Did God *really* say that?" Eve gave some to Adam who ate and ushered in the fall of man…a fall we are still suffering the effects of today.

Satan is still using the same games to distract, disarm, and destroy children of God. He hasn't changed. He is the same as he was in the beginning. The same serpent that whispered to Eve in the garden is still whispering today to our kids.

Who says you cannot do this? Who says you are not a boy or girl? Who says you must pick a gender when you can be both? Who says you can't love whom you want? Who says drugs are bad? Who says you can't take what you want…you deserve to have it. Who says God is real? Who says the stories your parents told you are true? Who says you must follow the Lord?

Lies. His lies place doubt in our kids and make them question God and His authority. Satan's tactics have not changed. They are the same as they were thousands of years ago.

If I was going to win the battle, I needed to be intentional every day with everything I did. My Bible reading, my worship, my thoughts, and the very words I spoke. This battle was gearing up, and I was about to report to duty for the first time in my Christian walk. I now realized I was in a war, but it was one I would not lose. I also knew many in the church were as asleep as I had been before awakening to the battle.

I had been guilty of going to a happy church and sitting around waiting for the rapture to get me out of here. I was ready to float away and forget the troubles of this world. My eyes were blinded. So many hurt, broken families needed restoration. One day, while praying, the Lord showed me how asleep the church was.

Our family loves puzzles. We often have one out on the table to put a few pieces in each day. And it never fails. You get to the end…almost all the pieces are in and you realize you're missing a piece. So we all have to search. Everyone is on the floor, trying to find the missing piece. Every shoe is lifted, every carpet hair combed, and every hiding place uncovered until that piece is found. The puzzle can't be finished until that piece is put in.

The Lord showed me that our kids are the last piece of that puzzle. The whole church is waiting for the glorious day of the return of Jesus when He comes and raptures the church and takes us home. We long for that day. We pray for that day. The problem is the puzzle isn't complete yet. The piece missing is our kids, and no one seems to care enough to go look for them. If we search so hard to make the picture on the puzzle complete, how much more should we be searching for the lost children of God?

I have been guilty of thinking I was ready, that it's not my problem if others aren't.

That is such a lie. The puzzle isn't complete if we all aren't home. We all need to get into this fight for families…for our children. Gone are the days of "oh, they'll come back."

Friends, our time is short. Jesus is coming and we need our kids to come home. We no longer have the luxury of time.

We must actively pray and search for the lost. We must stand with parents who have prodigal children. We must declare the Word of God over the lost.

It was time to develop a battle plan.

PRAYER

Lord, help me to know the hour in which we live…the time of Your soon return. Open my eyes to how late it is and help me feel the urgency to fight for a generation. Teach me to identify the enemy and to put the blame on him. Your Word says our battles are not against flesh and blood, but against Satan and his demons. Help me to stay focused not on earthly battles, but on the battle that is going on for the souls of our children. Help me to realize that Your coming is soon and the puzzle is not complete yet. Give me strength to continue the fight until every child is home. Show me how to pray and intercede for my family. In Jesus name.

SECTION 2
THE BATTLE PLAN

15. WHY A BATTLE PLAN?

I HAVE A FAVORITE COMMERCIAL. It's an insurance company, and the theme is, "It's what you do."

The commercial goes like this: A group of friends are running scared on a rainy night, away from a serial killer. They stop to gather their wits and figure out where to go next to be safe.

One says, "Let's go to the basement," and another says, "Why can't we get in the running car," which makes another person say, "Are you crazy? Let's go hide behind the chainsaws."

Then we see them running past the car that could take them to safety and instead, hiding in the most dangerous place.

The last scene of the commercial is my favorite. The serial killer is watching all of this. He takes off his mask and shakes his head. He's dumbfounded by the poor decisions these people make. The commercial ends with, "If you are in a horror movie, you make poor decisions. It's what you do."

Isn't that so true? I can just see God reacting the same way, watching us do the things we do. When we're in scary situations, He always shows us the way out. Yet, most of the time, we go hide behind the chainsaws, staying in a state of fear and doubt.

God never intended for us to fight our battles alone. He has already given us everything we need. He gave us His Word and His Holy Spirit. We're not alone. We don't have to sit back and fear the situation our kids are in, wondering what's coming next. All we need to do is open His Word and get our battle plan, then put on our armor and enter the war.

It's like God has given a running car to take us to safety!

A war is raging, my friends. A war for our kids, our family, and at times our very faith. If we're going to get into this fight and win the battles we face, we need a battle plan.

WHAT'S THE PLAN?

I realized early on, I needed concrete steps to help me fight this battle. I couldn't just get up every morning, randomly pick a few verses to read, listen to a few songs, and expect to push back the gates of hell.

There had to be a specific plan.

Months of praying and searching the Word led me to one that allowed me to take control, be active, seek, speak, and believe. The plan involves easy steps. Biblical steps. Steps we can find in the pages of Scripture. Steps that breathe life into dead bones.

Get in the fight, my friend. Don't sit on the sidelines any longer, buried by sadness and pain. Take back the power you've handed over to the enemy. He isn't in control of what our kids are doing. We'll fight and believe and declare truths and worship while doing it.

Maybe you're thinking, I have nothing to offer. I can't fight this. I'm just an ordinary mom.

Let me say right now that is a lie. God is not calling us because of what we offer. We are being called because of who He is and who we are in Him. If we are obedient to God in our ordinary lives, we can expect God to make an extraordinary impact. Our weakness is His strength. We only need to offer God what we have and see what happens.

I love the story of Elisha and his servant in 2 Kings.

The king of Aram was searching for Elisha, because Elisha would hear from God what Aram was going to do in battle against Israel and Elisha would warn Israel's king.

So, the king of Aram surrounded the town Elisha was in and his servant got really nervous. He went to Elisha, worried and scared about the great army with chariots and horses that were surrounding them. It meant certain defeat.

"He [Elisha] said, 'Do not be afraid, for those who are with us are more than those who are with them.' Then Elisha prayed and said, 'O LORD, please open his eyes so that he may see.' So, the LORD opened the eyes of the young man, and he saw, and behold, the mountain was full of horses and chariots of fire all around Elisha" (2 Kings 6:16–17).

Elisha knew. He walked so closely with God that he *knew* the battle belonged to the Lord. He didn't have to fear. He prayed a simple prayer…"O LORD, please open his eyes so that he may see." When He did, and the servant saw the truth. The army of the Lord outnumbered the enemy.

That is my prayer today. That the Lord would show us we are not alone in fighting for our families. I know it seems like the enemy has us outnumbered. It feels like the enemy is everywhere, after all our kids.

We must get a hold of who we are and the God we serve! The angel armies of God are with us fighting our battles. We are on the winning side!

We have to get into this war. We need to fight for our kids! Let us get our battle plan and get ready to fight!

There are five steps, and I'll break down each one.

16. DEVISING YOUR BATTLE PLAN

"FOR THE WORD OF GOD IS LIVING AND ACTIVE, sharper than any two-edged sword, piercing to the division of soul and of spirit, of joints and of marrow, and discerning the thoughts and intentions of the heart" (Hebrews 4:12).

If we are to win this war for our families, we have to put on our *armor* and get busy! In the following pages, I talk about ways we can *fight* this fight.

STEP 1: THE WORD

The first step is literally God's Word.

We are going to pick a battle verse—a verse you have picked or God has given you, to pray over your child. Pray for the truth you want to proclaim over them each day. I have a battle verse for my kids and when I don't have words to pray for them, I pray this verse.

There are 31,102 verses in the Bible. Start by asking God what truth to speak over your child. If there is a phrase or word that keeps coming to mind, start searching for a verse with that phrase and narrow it down to a few verses that speak to you.

Next, seek wise counsel from someone who can partner with you in prayer as you seek the Lord for your special verse.

Once you pick a verse, look for ways to use this in your daily life and prayers. Here are some ways I use this verse:

1. Memorize it! Commit this verse to memory and speak it aloud often.

2. Write it on index cards and place them around the house. Tape it to your bathroom mirror. Put it in the fridge so you see it each time you open the door. Put it under the cushions of your couch. Saturate every part of your house with the Word of God.

3. Make it your screensaver on your computer.

4. Put it next to your child's name on your phone. Every time they call, that verse will roll across the screen.

5. Put it on a card and place it under your child's mattress.

6. Put a picture of your child on a plastic sheet and write their verse on the back. Anoint that picture with oil daily and pray that verse over them.

7. Put it on your sun visor in your car.

8. If your child lives at home, pray the verse over their laundry as you do it.

9. If you have an Alexa in your house, ask her to read that verse. Speak it throughout your home.

10. Write it out on cards and hand them out to people who will pray with you.

These are just a few ideas to get you started. Use your imagination and come up with as many ways as possible to speak this verse over your child.

Isaiah 55:11 says, "So shall my word be that goes out from my mouth; it shall not return to me empty, but it shall accomplish that which I purpose, and shall succeed in the thing for which I sent it."

God will use this. His Word will not return to Him without changing us or our children. Your battle verse will be a powerful weapon in fighting for your children!

STEP 2: WORSHIP

My worship is my weapon!

You need a battle song.

Much like your battle verse, this is a song you sing over your child that reminds you of who God is, and it calms your soul when you are restless. I have a special song for each of my kids and when I hear it, I stop and just worship God for who He is and what He's doing. Music speaks when I don't have words. It centers me and ushers me into my secret place where I pour out my heart to the Lord.

When I am anxious, I put on that song and sing the words, reassuring my soul who my children belong to. I often put their names in the song as I'm singing. I could testify to being in the strangest places, feeling anxious, and hearing that special song out of nowhere. Pick a song and I promise you it will show up in the craziest places, always when you need to hear it.

In the story of the widow's offering in Luke 21:1–4...

"Jesus looked up and saw the rich putting their gifts into the offering box, and he saw a poor widow put in two small copper coins. And he said, 'Truly, I tell you, this poor widow has put in more than all of them. For they all contributed out of their abundance, but she out of her poverty put in all she had to live on.'"

How does this relate to worship? Worship comes naturally when everything in your life is going smoothly. It's effortless to put on worship music and thank God for His blessings. Attending church feels simple, and worship songs are straightforward to sing when all is well.

What's truly challenging is when you've lost everything. When you walk into church on a Sunday morning alone because your family is now broken, and yet you choose to lift your hands in praise. Like the widow who gave out of her poverty, our most sincere worship often comes from our own places of need.

When every ounce of faith we have left stirs our hearts to raise our hands to heaven, that deeply moves God's heart. Psalm 22:3 says, "Yet you are holy, enthroned on the praises of Israel."

God delights in our worship and receives it as an offering of praise. When we give out of our poverty of spirit, we're not giving from the abundance of our hearts, but from our emptiness. God sees our brokenness, and when we pour out our praise from that place, the gates of hell are shaken.

Choose a song that resonates with you and your situation. On those days when you're so broken you can't think straight, put on that song. Sing it over and over. Insert your child's name into it. Let the music express the words that won't come.

What songs will you pick? List your top three. Print out the words. Then, claim one as your battle song.

STEP 3: PRAYER

Part of doing spiritual battle is knowing what to pray, so the next step in coming up with a battle plan is figuring out what we specifically need to pray over our kids.

If we're going to push back the gates of hell, we're going to have to pray specific and effective prayers (James 5:16). We don't have time for the fluff anymore. Satan is after our kids, and it's time we boldly pray to break the strongholds. We need to exercise the authority given to us by Jesus to command the demons holding our children to flee.

Faith-filled prayer releases the power of God. There are so many things to pray for our kids. Here is a list to get you started.

1. Pray their own will for their lives would be broken and replaced with a desire to follow the will of God.

2. Pray their desire for the things of this world be replaced with a life led by the Spirit. Let nothing of their will work out. Let it be so obvious they would know that it was the hand of the Lord pointing them in the way they should go.

3. Pray for a heart to be broken over any part of their life not following the word of God. Pray the eyes of their heart to be opened, whatever the earthly cost. Not my will, but yours, Lord. We must love them enough to allow the pain of their sin to pierce their hearts and bring them to repentance.

4. Pray for God to reveal to you the spirit that has a hold on them and for the Lord's guidance in praying against that spirit. Use Matthew 18:18 as one of your guides.

5. Pray the Lord will give you a word of knowledge about anything in hidden in their hearts. Pray whatever they are dealing with would be brought out of the darkness and into the light. Pray that nothing will be concealed.

In Luke 22, Jesus tells Peter that Satan has asked for the right to sift him as wheat. But Jesus prays Peter's faith would not fail when the temptations come. Bind the enemy and pray your children will stand up to the schemes of the devil and their faith will not fail them.

Remind your kids you believe in them, regardless of the things they're saying or the things you're seeing. Say, "I am fighting for you, and I won't let Satan have victory in your life."

6. Pray against the influences manipulating them. Pray for God to remove toxic people in their lives and place a hedge of protection around them.

7. Pray God would put godly people in their lives.

8. Pray they would have a God wink each day…that they would see something, smell something, encounter someone who would remind them of their life in Christ.

9. Pray the godly seeds planted in them would grow. That the Holy Spirit would bring to their remembrance every verse ever memorized, every sermon they ever heard, every song they ever sang to help them in time of need (John 14:26).

10. Pray the scales on their eyes fall off and for God to give them eyes to see Him in every circumstance.

11. Pray for God to use our kids for *His* purposes (Jeremiah 29:11).

12. Pray for every single word written about them in heaven to come to pass. Pray they complete every assignment on this earth that God has for them (Ephesian 2:10).

13. Pray they will lead others to a saving knowledge of Jesus Christ.

14. Pray for your heart to trust God loves them so much more than you do.

15. Pray you will remain strong in faith, not wavering in be-

lieving your prodigal will come home. Pray for your humbleness before the Lord. If you want the Lord to bring your child to repentance, you must pray you are humble before him.

16. Pray to walk in the authority given to you in Jesus and through the power of the Holy Spirit. Bind what needs bound and loose what needs loosed.

17. Pray God will give you specific Scriptures for each child. Fill their names in while saying it.

18. Pray the Lord will raise up people in their workplaces who will point them back to Jesus.

19. Pray they can't go anywhere in public where they are not in contact with a follower of Jesus. That there is *no* way they can escape the godly influence on their lives.

20. Pray the Lord will give them visions and dreams to call them back to Him.

21. Pray they would have a Damascus Road experience and God would use whatever is necessary. Pray He would speak through a donkey if it were necessary.

If you are struggling with what to pray and how to pray, start with these things. If you have a hard time coming up with what to say, write out a prayer you can read. God hears every word!

STEP 4: DECLARATIONS

We are going to *declare* God's promises over our families. If there's one thing I've learned over the last few years, it is that there is power in my words. If I speak defeat, I will walk in defeat. If I speak the Word of God, there is life and hope! I choose life and hope!

- What are some of your favorite promises of God to declare over your family? Here are some of mine:
- Acts 16:31. Thank You, Lord, that if I believe, I and my household shall be saved.
- Luke 15:4. Thank You, Lord, that You leave the ninety-nine to go after the one.
- Isaiah 54:10. Thank You, Lord, that Your love never fails.
- James 1:5. Thank You, Lord, that you give wisdom to me when I ask.
- James 4:7. Thank You, Lord, that the Devil will flee from me when I resist.
- Deuteronomy 31:6. Thank You, Lord, that You will never forsake me or leave me.
- Psalm 50:15. Thank You, Lord, that when I call on You, you will answer.
- Hebrews 10:23. Thank You, Lord, that You are faithful.
- Thank You, Lord, for working in my prodigal's life.
- Thank You, Lord, that my child is a *man* (woman) of God and that he (she) is serving (claim the result) You with his (her) life.

Find ten favorite promises and declare them daily. Don't settle for defeat or listen to the enemy's lies. Declare with the authority of the God's Word what you know is true. Speak life over your family. It will move you from despair to victory!

STEP 5: COMMUNITY

You are not alone. Satan likes to whisper this journey is lonely, and you can't share your pain with anyone. That's a lie. You need friends to help you carry your prodigals to the feet of Jesus. You can't fight this battle by yourself. You need prayer warriors to believe in you, to help you lay your child before the Lord.

Just like in the story of the four friends and the paralytic, you need to find people who will help you carry the mat your child is on and lay them in front of Jesus. I think we can see the importance of having three helpers…one for each corner.

Ideally, these are local friends. Friends who can come over, hold you, pray with you, and hug you. These are people who know your heart for your family and will listen to your concerns. They are there for your good days and your worst days. We need mat carriers!

Identify who your mat carriers will be. Whom can you confide in to walk this journey with you? Who can be your phone-a-friend when you're having a bad day? With whom can you talk frankly, asking for help? Be brave. Speak up. Share your heart with those you are closest to.

Write three names of people you will ask.

Besides the mat carriers, we need an army fighting with us. We need intercessors in our corner who are lifting our children daily and believing for our prayers to be answered. Community is important to fight this battle. It's so important, I started a virtual community of moms who are believing in their children to come home.

It is called **Battle Cry Moms**.

Battle Cry Moms is a beautiful, deep community where we share the joys and sorrows, the good and ugly, the victories and defeats with one another. It is a place of no judgment and is comprised of imperfect moms and grandmas, sisters, and aunts. We all are unified under one banner, having those we love who have walked away and rejected the Lord Jesus Christ and our longing to see them return.

Our group comprises many types of parents going through different things, but all have the same cry of their heart…for their children to come to know the Lord Jesus Christ as their Savior. Why you need support doesn't matter. What matters is uniting to pray our children back to the loving arms of Jesus. Our motto is No One Fights Alone. Together we go to war against Satan and his demons, and we believe that *every last child will come home.*

I founded Battle Cry as an answer to the promise I made myself at the beginning of this journey. I couldn't fight this battle alone, but only with the help of others to carry my burdens and to carry me when I was too weak to go on.

The story of Moses, Aaron, and Hur in Exodus models this so well. In Exodus 17 the Israelites were at war with the Amalekites. As Moses held up his staff, the Israelites prevailed in the battle, but as his hands would fall, the tide of the battle would fall to Amalek.

Verse 12 says, "But Moses' hands grew weary, so they took a stone and put it under him, and he sat on it, while Aaron and Hur held up his hands, one on one side, and the other on the other side. So his hands were steady until the going down of the sun."

The intercessory help of his friends carried Moses through. It was their support that allowed him to push through to the end. Victory belonged to the Lord.

We are in the same place. We need each other. We have our arms up in a position of surrender, giving our children to the Lord. Yet, we grow tired. We grow tired in our flesh when what we see doesn't remotely look like a victory is coming. We need support that will come and hold up our arms when the battle is too much to bear alone. Satan knows there is victory when we stand together. That's why he tells us isolation is the only way.

But you are not alone. Stand with us, believing for our children to come home.

After the Israelites' victory, Moses built an altar and named the place Jehovah Nissi, The Lord Is My Banner. The banner was a pole-like standard raised over armies and communities. In ancient times, it was lifted to call the people together for battle. The phrase also means it was their battle cry. The victory was the Lord's. The battle was His.

The battle with our families is His too. He is fighting for us. We only need to stand together, holding up each other's arms as intercessory prayer warriors. The naming of the altar of Jehovah-Nissi is a reminder to us today that we can only be victorious as we honor the name of the Lord and rally to Him as our Banner.

Just as I had written in that first journal entry years ago…

The Devil comes to steal, kill, and destroy. He is trying to steal my peace, kill my children, and destroy my future. He will not succeed.

HE. WILL. NOT. SUCCEED.

Satan might think he has won, but this battle is just beginning. This battle is not against flesh and blood, but against Satan and his demons that come straight from hell. Demons that call our children out from their place at God's table and throw them into the darkness, far from the light. Yet, I believe. I believe even though I do not understand. I believe God has a plan and a purpose to use this. Get ready, Satan…you are in for a ride. You can go straight to hell because you LOSE…I read the end of the book!

This is my battle cry…LOVE GOES TO WAR.

We would love for you to join us in this fight. You can join at: BattleCryMoms.com.

17. FIX IT, JESUS

GROWING UP, I would run home from school to watch one of my favorite shows, *Gilligan's Island*. I looked forward to this each day.

It was the story of seven people who set off on an adventure that should have taken a bit of their afternoon. But when a storm approached, it threw them off course and they ended up shipwrecked on a deserted island. The show is all about the adventures that detour afforded them.

I loved tuning in each day to see what invention they made to make their lives easier or even who might drop by the island, yet never rescue them. It was the best show ever. It showed me detours in life do not always have to turn out to be disastrous, but they can be fun and create a life you didn't even know you ever wanted.

At the end of the show, they rescued the castaways. They spent time back in their old lives but what they all discovered was they did not like their old lives anymore. They longed for the new life that had been created through community, trust, and love.

I, too, have come to a place where I cannot unsee or unlearn the things God has taught me over the last few years and the lessons He is still teaching me. Had this off-road adventure not happened, I never would have learned new facets of God's character…facets I wouldn't have sought on my own. Being shipwrecked did not ruin their lives. It saved it. Walking this path has indeed not buried me, it projected me to what God had for me.

I heard a wonderful sermon the other day, based on the story of Joseph. I've been thinking a lot about it. We all know everything Joseph went through in his life, but it all led to the end when God used him to save many people. The focus, though, on this sermon was on Joseph's father, Jacob

Jacob loved his kids, but most of all, he loved Joseph. Now, I know we're not to have favorite kids, but Jacob did. It wasn't because of who Joseph was, but who his mom was. Joseph held a special place in Jacob's heart, and he had grand plans for Joseph as he grew.

The heartbreak is that Jacob lived his life thinking the worst…that Joseph had been killed. He grieved for this loss his whole life. Losing his plans for his family, his dreams, his entire future.

We know that pain, don't we, mama? We all had plans, dreams, mental images about what our lives were going to look like. Just like Jacob, our plans changed…and there is nothing we can do about it. We did not get a say in the detour life threw at us, and neither did Jacob.

But, just like Jacob, we trust God. It's easy to look at Jacob and this story and believe because we already know the end. It's on the pages of the Bible spelled out in words we can read. We can get lost in the middle of sadness, but keep on reading and we see redemption.

Oh, how I wish we could see this in our lives! I am stuck in the middle pages and I long to see the end of the story. My heart wishes it knew the happy ending…if it is going to be a happy ending. I am left with a lot of questions about why.

But there is one thing about Jacob's story I had never considered. God knew Jacob, and He knew his heart. If God had gone to Jacob and said, "Hey, I have this plan to save your family, actually a lot of families, but you're going to have to trust Me with your son. I am taking him from you and moving him to Egypt. Is that okay with you?"

Jacob would have said a great big *no*. You are *not* taking my kid! Find another family for Your plan. I am *not* giving up my son.

I wouldn't have given up mine either. If God had come to me almost seven years ago and said, "I am taking your son on a journey I have allowed, and it's going to be full of pain and loss for your family... and loss of your dreams. Are you okay with that?"

I would have put the brakes on right then and said nope! I am happy with where we are. Even if God revealed there would be good coming out of it, I wouldn't have allowed it. I would have held tight to my dreams and would never have agreed to this.

And there it was. In my heart, the hidden belief I controlled the outcome. I thought I could have my family and thank God—instead of thanking God and offering him my family.

I don't know the outcome for us. I don't know the result for you. But I have learned there is beauty in the ashes. Had I not been working through the pain and trusting God with my entire story, I would never have written this book or started a community of moms. I would have missed all *this*...and this is full of beauty!

I am so thankful God is taking all the broken parts of my life and making them into something beautiful.

In my Bible, Genesis 50:20 is at the bottom page 77. It says, "You intended to harm me, but God intended it for good, to..."

To what? What a cliffhanger!

How will I know what God has intended for this story? I have to turn the page. What happens when I find the strength to keep reading? I hear the rest of His plan. "To accomplish what is now being done, *the saving of many lives*" (emphasis mine).

I believe with all my heart our kids have a story. We are in the middle of it, but when we get a glimpse of the end, we will see the second part of that verse…the saving of many lives!

Nothing is wasted. God will use all this, and redemption will come. We must hold on and hold tight. *We must turn the page* and keep believing!

Turn the page today, mama! Believe your pain is planting a seed for the future…a future that is bright! I love you and I am praying for you all!

18. MOVING FORWARD

I HAVE A FAVORITE PICTURE of my kids. It's of them sitting and studying the map of Disney World. I had always wanted to go to Disney, and the time was finally coming. My lifetime dream was coming true. We were going to Florida, and we were taking the children on the vacation of a lifetime.

As best we could, we prepared for the trip. We sent off for the vacation videos from Disney. Each night, we watched them. We put the map on the wall and studied it, so we would know all the shortcuts to get to where we wanted to go. We watched videos of all the rides and decided on our must dos! This trip was exciting for us. We counted down the days with anticipation.

That, mama, is how we must wait for the day our kids come home. We must wait with anticipation. What does that look like to you? What will you do today to prepare for the glorious day your child comes home?

For me, it looks like this. I am going to plan the menu for the meal I will one day cook. I am going to buy the puzzle we will all sit at the table and do together. I am going to plan a vacation around the world that I am taking my grandkids on. I am going to wait with so much joy and anticipation of what I know God is going to do.

Sure, I'll be sad when the holidays roll around and our lives still look different from other families. I know the years I might be waiting will be hard, knowing holiday dinners are not what I wish they were. Yet I will not worry about any earthly meal. I am going to spend my time focusing on the only meal that matters—the Marriage Supper of the Lamb.

That is the only meal I care to make sure all my family is sitting at. Nothing else matters. Not a Christmas, a birthday, or Fourth of July picnic. I'll spend my days crying out for eternity for my family.

Wait with anticipation, mama. The Lord is at work, and it is His will that none should perish. He has our families, our hopes, and our dreams. He is working, and our job is to put on our armor and fight.

This is my battle cry…Love goes to war.

ABOUT THE AUTHOR

DEBRA MCNINCH is a child of the King, wife, mother, speaker, first-time author, and feeder of Butters, the neighborhood stray. She enjoys photography and working on her photo farm. Her four favorite things are Jesus, coffee, cupcakes, and glitter…in that order! She is a lover and collector of vintage junk, anything that sparkles, and all the sharpies! She prides herself on learning a new skill each year. She survives on God's Word and humor and loves when the two collide.

Debra is a Kansas girl at heart! She was born and raised in Winfield…home to Bluegrass and Burger Station. Her life has been full of adventure with nine family moves to six different states. Moving often has allowed her to see this amazing country, deepen her prayer life, and meet many dear friends.

Debra's first book, *Battle Cry: Waging the spiritual battle for your prodigal* was released by CrossRiver Media in Fall 2024. See writes and speaks about a parenting detour that led her to start the Battle Cry prayer movement, believing the prodigals are coming home. She started an online community made up of warrior moms believing for their children to return to a relationship with Jesus.

You can connect with Debra at DebraMcNinch.com.

"soul-searching"

"vulnerable"

UNCOVER YOUR
DIVINE
DESIGN

Who did God create you to be?

"highly recommend it!"

More great books from...
CrossRiverMedia.com

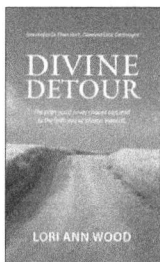

Divine Detour

Why trust a God who disappoints? A serious medical diagnosis took Lori Ann Wood on a faith detour she never saw coming. As a lifelong believer, she felt profound disappointment in the God she thought she knew. *Divine Detour* is the result of Lori Ann's risky decision to embrace difficult questions. Come along on a forty-day journey deep into the heart of a God who often doesn't behave as we'd like.

Hands Full

You know it. They know it. Everyone in the store knows it. You've got your hands full. In this humorous take on life and lessons learned living with her hands full, Brooke shares from her heart about her struggle to live out the fullness of her faith in the midst of the demands of motherhood and the redeeming love and grace available in Jesus. With His grace, we can empty these full hands into the hands of the One who holds the whole world.

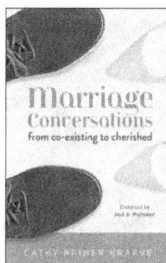

Marriage Conversations

Marriage requires serious communication. So, turn to the Master Communicator for strategies to soften hearts and strengthen resolve. Cathy will help you initiate practical, foundational truths; replace magical thinking with rock solid miraculous biblical truths; understand why we get married in the first place; and invigorate your closest relationship. Inspire the breathtaking relationship your heart is craving.

Books that build
battle-ready faith.

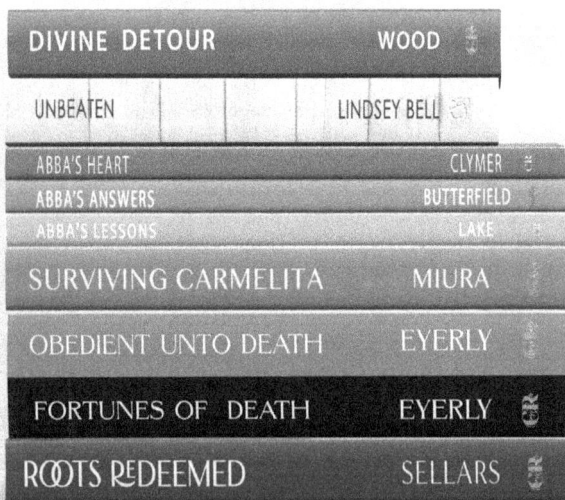

CR
Cross River

DIVINE DETOUR	WOOD
UNBEATEN	LINDSEY BELL
ABBA'S HEART	CLYMER
ABBA'S ANSWERS	BUTTERFIELD
ABBA'S LESSONS	LAKE
SURVIVING CARMELITA	MIURA
OBEDIENT UNTO DEATH	EYERLY
FORTUNES OF DEATH	EYERLY
ROOTS REDEEMED	SELLARS

If you enjoyed this book, will you consider sharing it with others?

- Please mention the book on Facebook, Instagram, TikTok, or another social media site.

- Recommend this book to your small group, book club, and workplace.

- Head over to Facebook.com/CrossRiverMedia, 'Like' the page and post a comment as to what you enjoyed the most.

- Pick up a copy for someone you know who would be challenged or encouraged by this message.

- Write a review on your favorite ebook platform.

- To learn about our latest releases subscribe to our newsletter at CrossRiverMedia.com.

www.ingramcontent.com/pod-product-compliance
Lightning Source LLC
LaVergne TN
LVHW051411080426
835508LV00022B/3032